The NEW ROI:

Return on Individuals

By Dave Bookbinder, ASA, CEIV

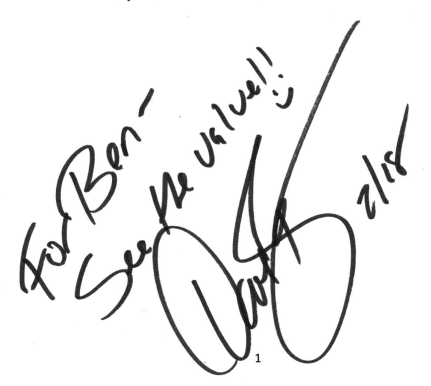

The NEW ROI:
Return on Individuals

Published by Limelight Publishing
7 Cattail Drive
Mount Laurel, NJ 08054-3087

ISBN: 978-0-9992371-0-6

DISCLAIMER AND/OR LEGAL NOTICES

While the publisher and authors have used their best efforts in preparing this book, they make no representations or warranties with respect to the accuracy or completeness of the contents of this book. The advice and strategies contained herein may not be suitable for your situation. You should consult a professional where appropriate. Neither the publisher nor the authors shall be liable for any loss of profit or any other commercial damages, including but not limited to special, incidental, consequential, or other damages. The purchaser or reader of this publication assumes responsibility for the use of these materials and information. Adherence to all applicable laws and regulations, both advertising and all other aspects of doing business in the United States or any other jurisdiction, is the sole responsibility of the purchaser or reader.

This book is intended to provide accurate information with regards to the subject matter covered. However, the Author and the Publisher accept no responsibility for inaccuracies or omissions, and the Author and Publisher specifically disclaim any liability, loss, or risk, whether personal, financial, or otherwise, that is incurred as a consequence, directly or indirectly, from the use and/or application of any of the contents of this book.

Table of Contents

Foreword

Successful CEOs, CFOs, and business owners are concerned about the return on every investment they make.

By its very nature, calculating the return on investment requires valuation metrics, never more critical than during the merger and acquisition process. Quantifying intangible assets, while not easy, is relatively simple compared to placing a value on what every CEO, CFO, business owner, or entrepreneur deems "the most valuable asset" in the organization – human capital.

Whether business leaders truly believe that their employees are their most valuable asset or are simply paying lip service to that line of thinking, understanding what that value is and how human capital affects the bottom line across every aspect of the company, from the C-suite to the shipping door, will make or break every organization.

Placing a value on human capital and the impact of the human capital on the value of a business is challenging but, as you'll discover, not necessarily impossible. Dave Bookbinder has always believed that people are an organization's most valuable asset and over the course of his career he's been uniquely positioned to observe that human capital has consistently been undervalued in M&A transactions for a variety of reasons, especially when compared to other intangible assets.

In following his gut feeling and dedicated to his belief that the human capital asset is undervalued, he began working to uncover a better, if not a quantifiable, method for reporting the true value of people and their impact on the value of an organization. The result of that effort is The NEW ROI: Return on Individuals.

This book, however, goes much further than unraveling a valuation formula. The true value of people is often founded in, and expanded by, corporate culture – another intangible and tough-to-define aspect of successful (or not-so-successful) organizations.

Many corporate leaders understand the cost of turnover and may even be able to enumerate it at a granular level. However, successful leaders understand that merely knowing the cost of turnover is like "locking the barn after the horse has bolted," proverbially speaking. The goal should be to not only avoid turnover in the first place, but to create a culture that embraces the value of employees that, in turn, increases the likelihood that those employees will arrive at work each day inspired to achieve greatness for both their organizations and themselves.

Cultivating trust, attracting difference makers, developing resilience and grit, valuing the rock star employees while limiting the toxic ones, building great teams, and nurturing positive attitudes, perspectives, and energy in the workplace all roll up to creating a valuable corporate culture and a valuable workforce. Dave and his team of collaborators explore each of these components and more throughout this book.

Even if in the end, it is in fact, impossible to place a finite, quantifiable value on human capital assets, it is clear that people have a tremendous impact on a company's value, and doing what it takes to develop and maintain a great corporate culture will always fall to the bottom line.

Charles Weinstein, CEO
EisnerAmper LLP

Introduction
The NEW ROI: Return on Individuals

Here's a story about a real company:

This company provided doughnuts for its software development team every day. Good doughnuts – and a great assortment of them, too.

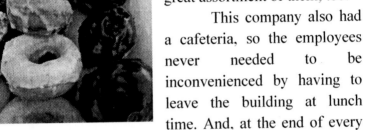

This company also had a cafeteria, so the employees never needed to be inconvenienced by having to leave the building at lunch time. And, at the end of every day, employees were given a free pot-luck dinner.

Sounds like a pretty good company – want to work there? Sure, why not?

And now, for the rest of the story....

The company's motivations in providing these perks weren't exactly altruistic. You see, management learned that the software developers were willing to arrive at work an hour or more ahead of their scheduled reporting time to get the best pick of the doughnuts. First come, first served.

The assortment was also purposefully designed to create urgency as nobody wanted to get stuck with the few deliberately less desirable doughnuts that were always included in the assortment.

Regarding lunch, management believed that productivity would suffer if employees went out to eat.

Having an in-house cafeteria discouraged employees from leaving the building, plus they'd spend less time on lunch breaks.

The dinner announcement came between 6:30 and 7:00 p.m. The design was to get employees to stay beyond the end of their normal work day. And the free pot-luck dinners? They were the items that weren't eaten at lunch time and would likely be discarded anyway.

How do you feel about this company now? Did they value their employees? Still want to work there?

The WHY Behind This Book

As someone who's regularly involved in the valuation of intangible assets, I'm often asked which intangible asset is the most valuable to a company. I've always believed that it's the people. But sometimes it's just hard to quantify exactly what that value is.

And as someone who has tried to quantify the value of people for a large part of my career, I can tell you it's usually the other intangibles, like patents or trademarks that mathematically wind up proving to be more valuable assets. Why? Simple. They're *more* quantifiable. While there *are* formulas on how to value people, they do not tell the whole story.

A few years ago, I was introduced to a fellow named David Jardin, founder of the Integrated Talent Management System, because we both "valued people." David believed that all too often, the contributions of the workforce were not fully understood by management teams who relied on ineffective ways to measure such things.

He believed that with the right talent management tools in place, employee engagement and productivity would increase and that management teams could have that ah-ha moment of realization that the employees can make a real difference – and in a measurable way. A quantifiable way that would lead to an assessable value like the other intangibles any company may have. A measurement that could be reported on a financial statement, if you will.

We began to collaborate on how our respective worlds "value" people; where in the valuation world, "to value" typically refers to "quantifying the worth of" while in the talent management world, "to value" typically referred to "being appreciated." Our respective worlds simply embraced the alternate definitions of the word:

Value: noun | val-ue | \ 'val-(,)yü\ :
- *The amount of money something is worth*
- *Usefulness or importance*

Our intuition was that there was likely a high correlation to a valued (i.e., appreciated) workforce having tremendous value, in dollars and cents on the bottom line. But how could we prove that?

We believed that if we could marry the disciplines of valuation and talent management, we could change the way people are evaluated, change the way leadership perceives their employees, and quantify the impact of both on the overall value of the business.

The hope was to identify a mathematical equation – the secret formula – to make such a determination.

Unfortunately, David passed away before we were able to pursue this fully; however, he inspired me to continue the conversation with others in an effort to keep the dream alive. And the more people I talked to about this project, the more people wanted to be a part of it.

This book is the collection of the series titled, "The NEW ROI: Return on Individuals," that documents my quest to find greater meaning in the context of valuing people and the contribution of people to the value of an enterprise. However, this book is also only the starting point. I realized as I continued to work to unravel the

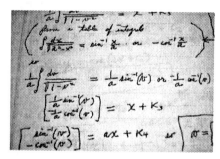

concept and attempt to create that secret formula, developing the correlation between business valuation and talent management, my quest may possibly be unending.

To be clear from the outset, I'm not writing this book as an HR consultant nor as a business coach of any sort. Ask anyone in management what the business's most valuable asset is and the answer will always be a resounding, "The people!" Yes, people drive the value of any business, but that workforce never makes it on to the financial statements. It's an intangible asset but is also far more nebulous than other intangibles like intellectual property, trademarks, patents, and customer relationships.

Throughout this book, I'll be sharing the data that I've uncovered and the conversations that I've had in collaborating with various thought leaders throughout North America. Some chapters include re-prints of articles written by my collaborators on this project.

Some of the things we will cover include:

- The Characteristics of a Difference Maker
- The Impact of Attitude and Perspective
- The Science of Teaming
- The Importance of Trust for Innovation
- The Impact of Happiness on Productivity
- The Cost of Toxic Employees
- The Real Return on Investment in Human Capital

At the end of this book, I hope that we'll get feedback from readers who find that some of the messages resonated with them. Perhaps some readers will even continue in the ongoing and constantly unfolding conversation on the topic. I hope to provide a synthesis of the various perspectives and present a road map for how to maximize the value of your most important assets – people… and just maybe, provide a secret formula to help to quantify that value. At the very least, I hope that the information we're about to cover will broaden your perspective and put an exclamation point to the concept that, quantifiable or not, people are truly the most important asset of any business and that value ultimately drives success across the board – oftentimes in the increased valuation of the enterprise!

Note: Links to referenced studies, data, and further reading, etc. are included in the Resource section at the end of the book.

Introduction

Chapter One:

The Value of the Workforce

With Chris Mercer and Jeff Higgins

"People are our most valuable assets," said every chief executive officer of every company everywhere. Right?

But how do you really know that's the case? Or is it mere lip service that sounds good to employees and stock holders?

Power to the People

In manufacturing, at the end of the day or shift, the majority of the assets (e.g., the equipment and machines) stay right where they are. However, in professional services businesses, the assets pack up and go home every night. Yes, there are tangible assets in professional services businesses (computers, software programs, diagnostic equipment, etc.) that stay put as they do in manufacturing. However, in fields like legal, engineering, architectural, medical, and accounting, for example, where the *expertise of the people* is really what customers, clients, and patients are buying, the employees are clearly the main assets of the business. What they are producing is an intangible product. Yes, there might be a tangible blueprint or a tax return, but the tangible product in this case simply represents the expertise of the employee or workforce that created it. The real value is in their brain power.

(This is certainly not to suggest that the workforce in the manufacturing sector is less important, and certainly those machines and equipment need skilled, talented operators; however, the end result is truly a tangible product to be sold and is designed and accounted for as such.)

The people working in professional services are measured based on certain metrics like utilization rates (the number of hours billed / number of hours worked) and

realization rates (actual fees collected / budgeted fees). In businesses where products are manufactured or distributed, the people (or human capital assets as they are often referred to) are just one of many assets. In professional services, the human capital assets are the primary assets. Tangible assets in these businesses exist to support their expertise.

Each employee's direct contribution to sales and profits is different, and it is even more difficult to document their performance with quantitative metrics –

especially for those who are not directly responsible for sales. Once you get past the measurables like attendance, or some number of projects completed, it's often a more subjective assessment process.

While there are convenient statistics to measure productivity, these numbers don't tell the whole story about an individual's contributions or the value that they bring to an organization.

People Are Intangible Assets

When folks in my profession talk about determining the value of people, it is typically in the context of a business combination that's called a purchase price allocation (PPA). The PPA is an accounting exercise that requires the assignment of the fair value of all tangible

Although quite valuable, the assembled workforce asset is not actually booked on a financial statement. Rather, it is recorded as a part of goodwill.

and intangible assets and liabilities acquired in a business acquisition.

Human capital is considered to be an intangible asset and a common way of ascribing value to people is through the assembled workforce in its entirety. The existence of a highly trained workforce in place saves an acquirer from having to go out and recruit, hire, and train a new group of employees to effectively operate the business.

In calculating the value of the workforce, valuation practitioners will often use a Cost-to-Recreate method. The math behind the methodology is such that if we can estimate all of the costs incurred to recreate the workforce, that total cost will reasonably represent the *value* of the workforce.

For example, if "Ed in Accounting" costs $75,000 (salary, benefits, recruitment, training, etc.), the methodology presumes that we can find, hire, and train another person just like Ed for the same $75,000.

According to Jeff Higgins, Chief Executive Officer of the Human Capital Management Institute, in this example, Ed's salary of $75,000 might be below-market. Jeff notes, "People figure out talent arbitrage really well. They know who are the good people to work for and who are the managers to avoid, and they will oftentimes accept a lower salary to work in the right environment with the right people."

So in a Cost-to-Recreate model, we might already be understating the value of the workforce to the extent that replacing Ed might actually cost more than his current salary would suggest.

Before I continue, I want to be very clear that this is not a criticism of how valuation practioners go about valuing human capital or how the accounting profession recognizes that asset. Intellectually, we are simply valuing a particular asset in a particular way using the tools and methods that are available and accepted.

My observation is, however, that when valuing the workforce, some implicit shortcomings in the Cost-to-Recreate method come to the surface. First is the assumption that all employees are interchangeable – that is, one Ed is just as good as another Ed in the same way that one computer or other piece of equipment is the same as and just as good as another.

The second is that cost and value are one and the same. Lastly, the Cost-to-Recreate method focuses largely on only the *direct* costs associated with replacing people but never accounts for the impact they make to the company's bottom line.

Chris Mercer, Valuation Expert and CEO of Mercer Capital, agrees with these observations. Regarding valuing human capital via the Cost-to-Recreate method, Chris states, "It captures a cost, but the value of people is really the benefit that they bring... and if the value of an employee didn't exceed the cost to hire them, they probably wouldn't have been hired in the first place."

Applying Chris's thinking and using Ed as an example, Ed's value to the company far exceeds what appears on his resume, so the cost of replacing him isn't simply a matter of finding someone else with similar education and experience. Besides his thorough accounting knowledge, Ed also fully understands the organization's clients and has a thorough knowledge of its history. He can leverage this knowledge to boost the company's bottom line. Ed brings benefits to his employer that will likely take his replacement weeks, months, or possibly years to replicate.

The High Cost of Turnover

Inherent in Chris's observation is that there is more to the story than simply the cost associated with replacing people. Certainly, more than just the direct costs.

According to data released by the Center for American Progress, the direct cost associated with turnover for an average employee is roughly 20 percent of annual salary. For more specialized personnel and executive-level employees, the costs can exceed 200 percent.

There are also, however, indirect costs associated with replacing employees that aren't fully captured in the statistics. Such things include:

- The lack of productivity that the employee exhibits once they've made the decision to disengage;
- The impact on remaining employees' morale as they question the reasons behind the departures/termination; and
- The real cost of lost productivity.

The real cost of lost productivity refers to the fact that while estimates can be made regarding when a new employee comes up the learning curve to a reach a satisfactory level of performance, it doesn't account for the replacement of the nuanced things that longer-term employees have learned over time. Things like corporate culture and protocols; the best resources within the company for specific information; and even the boss's preferences. Call it institutional knowledge, and it truly impacts productivity. More importantly, the employees with institutional knowledge are valuable assets.

According to the Society for Human Resource Management (SHRM), perhaps the largest indirect cost is the impact of departures on the disruption of the talent pipeline. SHRM estimates the inclusion of indirect costs to employee turnover to be between 100 and 300 percent of the annual salary. There's also the opportunity costs of replacing an employee – a bad hiring decision can cost up to *five times* that employee's salary according to SHRM.

According to Jeff Higgins, "Management's focus should be on sustainable productivity. The 'do it or else' model may yield short-term results but will actually under-perform in the long run due to the high cost of turnover of working for that type of manager."

> *"The way in which appraisers attempt to determine the value of a workforce-in-place can't capture the value of what people do for an organization."*
> ~ *Chris Mercer*

Who hasn't made, at one time or another, a bad hiring decision? It's probably a far more expensive mistake than anyone realizes.

Employees Are Individuals

We know that all employees are not identical, and not all employees are average. Within the category of above-average to excellent are the difference makers within the organization. I'm talking about the positive difference makers. (We'll get to the negative ones, also.)

So what are the characteristics of these positive difference makers in an organization?

On to the next chapter.

Chapter Two:

The Difference Makers

Attitude is everything.

Or is it?

Great attitudes are infectious and can positively impact the behaviors of others. Of course, poor attitudes can also be infectious... and not in a good way, but that's a subject for another chapter.

So when we think about what defines a positive difference maker, is it really all about attitude?

In the last chapter, we discussed the valuation technique used to value the assembled workforce. We made the observation that people are not fungible and are not commodities that can be traded or substituted. Recall that "Ed in accounting" is not the same as every other accountant and you cannot simply replace Ed with another Ed. There's more to think about than only the cost of replacement when assessing the value of employees. We also noted that within the aggregated workforce there are difference makers.

So what defines a difference maker?

In author and speaker, John Maxwell's book, *The Difference Maker*, he busts the myth that "attitude is everything" and explains that while attitude is important, it is not, in fact, everything.

There are certain things that attitude alone cannot overcome. A good attitude isn't a substitute for experience. Attitude also can't overcome a lack of skill nor can it overcome certain facts. In other words, despite my love of hockey and desire to play in the NHL, the fact that I am past the prime age of a typical hockey player and lack the skill to even ice skate prevent me from living that dream. My positive attitude about wanting to play ice hockey will make not one whit worth of difference in actually being able to do so.

That said, Maxwell writes that attitude is a primary component in determining success. He explains that attitude is the difference maker in how we approach and deal with relationships and challenges. It might be the one single thing that we always have in our control, regardless of the circumstances.

Since it's not attitude alone, what then makes people become difference makers and ultimately more valuable to their organizations?

Studies conducted by OC Tanner Institute, including research conducted with Forbes Insight, were published in the book entitled *Great Work*. In summary, it describes the mindset of people who achieve noteworthy results as follows:

> *"If you don't like something change it. If you can't change it, change your attitude."*
> ~ *Maya Angelou*

"Great difference makers shift from seeing themselves as workers with an assignment to crank out, to seeing themselves as people with a difference to make."

So difference makers have the attitude that they are, in fact, difference makers.

The results of a study of roughly 1.7 million people across all industries found that what sets these high performers apart isn't a set of traits like intelligence or ambition. Difference makers, or high performers, simply do things differently at work.

The five specific things that difference makers do to achieve better results are:

1) They Ask the Right Questions

Difference makers ask things like, "Why does this take so long?" "Why can't we..." "What if ..." Difference makers are not going to be satisfied with a "that's the way we've always done it" answer and mentality.

2) They See How Things Work

Difference makers look at work in ways that others haven't. They recognize the importance of seeking to understand the work from the recipient's point of view. This perspective allows them to better tailor their deliverables for the recipient.

3) They Have Out-of-Network Conversations

Difference makers regularly talk to people outside their immediate network of friends and associates. They understand that their immediate networks have a high correlation with similar contacts who might look at issues through similar lenses or experiences. By going outside of their network, difference makers will build on the ideas that result from this variety of perspectives. Going out of network helps them, well, see things differently.

4) They Improve Things

Difference makers are looking to develop new techniques and strategies and to optimize processes or products. For a difference maker, there are always possibilities. "Good enough" is never good enough. Difference makers are the ones who are always building better mouse traps.

5) They Take Ownership

Difference makers don't pass the buck or hold the belief that something is "not my job." Difference makers take great pleasure from the sense of accomplishment. This feeling inspires them to take on even more difference-making endeavors, and the upward-spiral continues.

So when it's all said and done, a great attitude is only one characteristic of a difference maker.

Chapter Three:

Want to Be Successful? Here's the One Thing You'll Need

Why do some really smart people fail where other, less intelligent people succeed?

It's simple: being smart isn't enough.

Sure, talent and skill are very important, and as we've already discussed in the last chapter, a great attitude cannot compensate for the lack of either of those. So what does it take to be successful?

In the last chapter, we discussed the five things leaders look for in a difference maker. We covered the distinguishing characteristics of difference makers and how they think and act that sets them apart from everyone else, like asking the right questions, seeing how things work, looking outside of their own networks, making improvements, and taking ownership. So now, we're going to explore a particular personality trait of difference makers and an important key to success known as Grit.

What Exactly Is Grit?

Dr. Angela Lee Duckworth is professor of psychology at the University of Pennsylvania and author of the book, *GRIT – The Power of Passion and Perseverance.* Dr. Duckworth's work is part of a growing area of psychology research focused on non-cognitive skills. The term non-cognitive skills refers to a set of attitudes, behaviors, and strategies that are thought to underpin success at school and at work, such as motivation, perseverance, and self-control.

In other words, it includes the characteristics other than intelligence that contribute to human development and success.

In her TED Talk, Dr. Duckworth describes Grit as much more than simply the notion of dedication and commitment. Grit is "having passion and perseverance for long-term goals." In fact, Dr. Duckworth's research suggests that Grit is the distinguishing characteristic of high achievers in every field.

> *"Grit is living life like it's a marathon, not a sprint."*
> ~ Angela Lee Duckworth

When it comes to high achievement, Grit may be every bit as essential as intelligence. And while intelligence can be easily measured, intelligence alone doesn't explain an individual's success. For example, you probably know smart people who aren't high achievers, and conversely, you probably know people who achieve great things without having had the best grades. (Think: Albert Einstein and Henry Ford.)

The research suggests that the difference is due to high achievers possessing Grit.

What Does Grit Look Like?

Talent without Grit is simply wasted potential. Combine talent with Grit and you've got the making of a superstar.

Think of any exceptional athlete or musician. For example, by the year the Beatles burst onto the international scene, the band had already played over 1,200 concerts together. By comparison, most bands today don't play 1,200 times in their entire careers.

Without the Grit to practice their skills while others were watching TV or hanging out with friends, they wouldn't have achieved their levels of success. And let's face it: their level of success is undeniable and changed the face of music in many ways. Whether or not they knew it or perhaps called it by something else, the Fab Four had Grit.

Grit is associated with an optimistic explanatory style and growth mindset. By definition, an explanatory style is how people explain to themselves why they experience a particular event as either positive or negative. For example, when something bad occurs, pessimists will tend to blame themselves for it while optimists will almost always chalk it up to simple bad luck. (More to come on positive psychology in a subsequent chapter). Gritty individuals tend to follow through on their commitments. Gritty individuals also have a strong sense of purpose and are motivated to find happiness through focused engagement.

Oftentimes, successes come from simply showing up – especially when others don't. And while there are plenty of tools to predict the performance of the individuals who do show up, these tools are usually poor predictors of the willingness and ability to show up in the first place.

> *"80 percent of success is showing up."*
> *~ Woody Allen*

Meet one of the collaborators on this book and project, Dave Nast of Nast Partners. Dave is both a believer in, and an example of, Grit. He tells a story of how he started running at age 35 and within two months had five stress fractures in his left foot which left him in a cast for four months.

His doctor told him that his build was more "football player than runner" and that he should give up running and consider cycling for less impact. But Dave did not give up – he was determined to accomplish his goal of running a marathon.

Three years later, after completing his third marathon, Dave sent the doctor a thank-you note for getting him back on his feet and for the motivation. You see, being told he couldn't do something made Dave even more determined. Dave wound up joining a running club, talked with experienced runners, and read books about distance running. He followed training plans, set goals, and achieved them.

As Dave says: "Setting goals and tracking your progress is a sign of Grit – and you can't take 'grit' out of integrity."

> *Grit | Noun: COURAGE, bravery, pluck, mettle, backbone, spirit, strength of character, strength of will, moral fiber, steel, nerve, fortitude, toughness, hardiness, resolve, resolution, determination, tenacity, perseverance, endurance; informal: guts, spunk.*

To Dave's point, the characteristics of integrity, like being good to your word, performing to the best of your abilities, and owning your mistakes, all speak to the characteristic of Grit.

If you're wondering how you measure Grit, you can take a very brief test at www.angeladuckworth.com/grit-scale/ to see where you fall on the "Grit Scale." (My score was 4.70; what's yours?)

Dr. Duckworth notes that while this test is self-reported and therefore possibly open to gaming, what she has found is that a person's Grit score is highly predictive of achievement under challenging circumstances.

Want to Be Successful? Here's the One Thing You'll Need

Chapter Four:

How Great Leaders Keep Top Performers Happy and Productive

With Marla Tabaka (As it appeared in **Inc.** *magazine)*

A disengaged work force can destroy a company's value. Invest in the difference makers, and you will see a remarkable ROI.

When asked what their company's number one asset is, smart leaders will answer that it's their employees. Yet a whopping 50 percent of employees who leave a company do so because of their relationship with the boss.

There are obvious consequences in lacking a culture that embodies positive company values and due appreciation of its employees. Valuation expert Dave Bookbinder sheds a new light on the importance of such a culture in a series of articles he's publishing called "The NEW ROI: Return on Individuals."

"It's no secret that a happy work force is a more engaged work force, and a more engaged work force is a more productive work force," writes Bookbinder. "It's important to recognize that the people are responsible for translating that productivity into an increased value of the overall business enterprise. Conversely, a disengaged work force can destroy a company's value."

How can you build this value into your company's overall worth? "In the valuation world, where people are referred to as human capital assets, it's the positive difference makers, or high performers, who are the greatest asset," Bookbinder says. Difference makers are the ones who ask the right questions, see the whole picture, and go outside of their networks to gather ideas from a variety of

perspectives. Difference makers know that good enough is never good enough. And since they get great pleasure from a sense of accomplishment, they take ownership of every project they touch.

According to Bookbinder, retaining these difference makers will help you, not only in the short term, but also in successfully implementing your long-term strategy. Building value now will pay off in the future.

Here are some of the things that are most important to difference makers. Build a culture that allows them the opportunity to make a difference, and your top performers will remain happy and productive for years to come.

1. Understand their goals.

Take the time to discover their personal goals and find a way to tie them into the goals of the organization. For example, if someone has aspirations to start a business, allow him or her to pursue entrepreneurial endeavors inside the company. By aligning the individual's goals with those of the company, you will turn a mercenary (someone who works for the top dollar) into a missionary (someone who believes in and is loyal to the organization).

2. Invest in them.

Professional development, training, and coaching are investments, not perks. If you view people as expenses, they will behave accordingly. Human capital is an asset after all, even if it doesn't show up on a financial statement. An average CEO may ask, "What if we invest in our employees and they leave?" An outstanding CEO will ask, "What if we don't invest in our employees and they stay?"

3. Create a connection.

Difference makers are looking to make a deep connection with not only their work, but also the people they work with and work for. If you are a managing a difference maker, adopt a leadership style that resonates with him or her. Your actions must be in alignment with your words. Remember, these people don't quit their jobs, they quit their bosses.

4. Develop the stakes beyond salary, benefits, and perks.

For difference makers, it's about more than money – it's about meaningful work and being a part of something bigger than the task at hand. Yes, the compensation package has to be appropriate, but allow your difference makers to ask their probing questions and identify areas that need improvement without being judgmental. If you let them have at it, there is a good chance that they will improve upon it.

5. Surround them with high-caliber colleagues.

Just as no single great athlete can make a team successful, difference makers also need to be surrounded by talented players. Allow your top talent to collaborate and reap the exponential benefits of that collaboration.

All in all, your top performers are inspired and motivated by internal factors, not external ones. They're not the people who are just working in wait for the weekend to come. By creating this type of culture, you might just inspire a whole new group of difference makers that you didn't even know you had.

Chapter Five:

In Search of the Purple Squirrel

With Dave Nast

The purple squirrel is a mythical creature.

Similar to unicorns, purple squirrels exist only in the imagination. Despite that, you will want one, so you need to know how to find one.

The term purple squirrel is often used in reference to describing those hard-to-find, rock star employees who we've been referring to as difference makers. The employees who drive the value of an organization.

In the last chapters, we covered the definition of the difference makers and ways to keep them happy… and retain them! So, yes, you want to keep those difference makers –  those purple squirrels – in your organization, but now it's time to delve into the process of finding and attracting them in the first place.

To gain some insight on how to go about doing this, I once again talked with Dave Nast of Nast Partners.

According to Dave, things like best-in-class products and services or leading brands can attract top tier candidates initially. Great benefits, flexible hours, stock options, equity, swag, and a lifestyle that speaks to work-life balance are all expected as the bare-minimum requirements if you truly want to attract the cream of the crop.

But, Dave says, "Savvy difference makers know how to research and network any potential employer. In this age of transparency, they will find current and former employees on LinkedIn and network with industry insiders to get the scoop on what it's really like to work there."

So, the thing that actually attracts a difference maker is... other difference makers. The ones who *evangelize* throughout the industry, market, and their own networks.

As we discussed previously, difference makers desire organizations that will invest in their professional development through training, coaching, tuition reimbursement, and other benefits. Top performers also tend to get bored easily, so they are attracted to opportunities that will keep them challenged, learning, and on the cutting edge of their industry and function. They are drawn to corporate cultures in which they will be regularly recognized, whether it is through unexpected or discretionary bonuses, awards, and/or announcements and credit and acknowledgment.

As a former headhunter, Dave views the selection of best-fit candidates as a mad alchemy of art and science. The art of selection is the skill acquired over years of experience, so let's talk about the science.

The Science of Selection

When it comes to identifying the difference makers from the rest of the crowd, Dave believes that behavioral interviews have fallen out of fashion and proven not to be predictive of performance. Candidates who are skilled at improvisation tend to ace these types of interviews that have questions that begin with, "What would you do if...?"

Competency-based interviews are in vogue and focus on the background, experience, skills, and knowledge of the candidate. These types of interviews have questions that begin with,  "Tell me about a time when...?" which begs for real stories and experiences. The competency-based interview gets at what is in the candidate's "briefcase," so to speak. This is better; however, it's only predictive of performance six percent of the time!

When you add a behavioral assessment to the interview, it becomes 23 percent predictive of performance. The behavioral assessment functions to get at what is in the candidate's heart rather than what may simply be in his or her "briefcase." When we start getting at what's in a candidate's heart, we're starting to learn the level of Grit they may possess as well.

Finally, when you add a cognitive assessment to determine what is in the candidate's head, you're making real progress. Coupled with the behavioral assessment, it becomes 51 percent predictive of performance.

So, the key to hiring difference makers is to gain access to their head, heart, and briefcase during the selection process. The use of Psychometric Analytics in hiring has been in fashion for a while now. But, like fashion, what's old is new again.

According to Dave, the leading solution – and the only one validated to be used for hiring and selection – is The Predictive Index© (PI). PI is 60 years old, but there's a  lot that's new as millions of dollars have been injected into the solution. With over 500 validation studies, 8,000 customers, and more than 2.5 million people taking PI each year, it is one the most scientifically valid and reliable solutions for hiring.

Dave adds: "Data is good, but as a guy who's placed over 500 CEOs in my day, I think about the candidate experience. Top performers and difference makers who are in high demand don't want to spend hours taking a bunch of assessments."

PI only takes about five minutes to complete and provides more than just best-fit selection statistics. What differentiates PI is that the user can create something called Performance Requirement Options (PRO). This is essentially a job profile for the candidate.

The ideal game plan would be to administer this to your difference makers to determine the optimal candidate profile of what it takes to be a top performer in a given role. Reverse engineering it, in a matter of speaking. The more difference makers who take the PRO, the more accurate it will be.

The software then synthesizes the results of the individual PROs from the various difference makers and creates a unified PRO for what is required to be a difference maker. Then when the PI is administered to all new candidates, it will match the candidate's PI against the "difference maker PRO" that was created to scientifically validate whether or not the particular candidate  possesses the characteristics of a difference maker. In other words, it will help reveal whether or not the candidate is a purple squirrel.

The system will also generate the appropriate competency-based interview questions to ask, taking the guess-work out of which competencies to delve into during the interview. But it doesn't end there.

It will also generate coaching questions based on their PI's match to the PRO, so it can predict where the candidate might excel and where they might struggle. So, after hiring the new difference maker, their manager will know which questions to ask in order to help them succeed and how best to keep them engaged in the future... exactly what the difference maker, the purple squirrel, wants.

Dave says: "If you can improve the communication and understanding of the individual drivers between the employee and manager, you can increase the likelihood of hiring success and ultimately, retention. That, of course, will impact a company's valuation."

And ultimately improve the likelihood of building a team of purple squirrels.

Chapter Six:

How to Value the Rock Stars

They walk into a meeting like Bruce Springsteen taking the stage for his first encore. They collaborate like Lennon and McCartney. They possess the creativity of Prince, and they've got the moves like Jagger.

They are your rock star employees.

They can be found in every area of the organization. For some, their job titles might suggest that they are "backup singers" or even "roadies," but you know that they are rock stars, and their absence would be felt (and painfully so) if they were to leave your "stage."

Rock Star Valuation

You might recall from an earlier chapter (The Value of the Workforce) that the valuation methodology used to determine the value of the assembled workforce doesn't quite tell the whole story about the contributions that 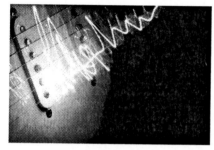 people make to the value of an organization. You'll remember that people, despite having similar job titles and resumes, are not simply interchangeable.

When thinking about how to value the rock stars of an organization, it gets even fuzzier. Here's why...

Unless the rock stars are directly responsible for an activity that results in a measurable economic outcome, it is very difficult to quantify their contributions to the organization. In the world of valuation, a rock star employee is typically identified as someone who is bound by a non-competition agreement. That agreement's existence underscores the desire to keep the employee. (Employees without non-competition agreements are seen as a bit more disposable or, at least, don't create the threat of negative economic impact should they land with a competitor or strike out on their own in the same business.) However, even in circumstances in which measurable economic outcomes do exist, we still can't directly attribute that value to the rock star employee.

The reason, as we've previously discussed, is that human capital assets are not recorded on financial statements, so one of the ways that a valuation analyst might determine the value of a rock star employee is by *inference* if the employee is bound by a non-competition agreement. It's captured by inference because it's the non-competition agreement that might get booked on the financial statements, not the person.

The Non-Competition Agreement

The non-competition agreements or "Non-Competes" as they are called, are legal, marketing-related intangible assets that are entered into when an employee is hired or when the employee is on-boarded as a result of coming over in an acquisition. Oftentimes, the employees that are bound by Non-Competes are more senior in rank and have responsibility for sales, customer or supplier relationships, or have a particular knowledge with regard to intellectual property.

Because of these relationships and/or unique knowledge, if these employees were to leave their current

employer and start a competing business or join a

competitor, the current employer could suffer economic damages in the form of lost sales and profits. The Non-Compete affords the company some protection against that outcome. The Non-Compete goes into effect from the time an employee leaves the company (voluntarily or involuntarily) through a typical term of one to five years. It may also prevent the employee from competing within a certain geographic radius during that term as well.

The methodology used to value the Non-Compete quantifies the present value of the economic damages resulting from the hypothetical departure of the rock star. In other words, if the person was not bound by the Non-Compete and they had the ability and desire to compete, we can quantify the economic damage that they could do to the company if they did compete.

What Are the Odds?

But we don't stop there. After determining the total magnitude of the economic damages that could be caused by the departure of the rock star employee and subsequent hiring by a competitor or launching a competing business, the valuation methodology necessitates that consideration be given to the *probability* of successful competition.

In estimating the probability of successful competition, valuation experts give consideration to the employee's ability to raise the necessary capital to start their own business, for example. We then consider how long it would take to get that new operation up and running to the point of being able to compete. We also consider the alternative that an existing competitor within a reasonable commuting distance of the employee might be a more viable scenario for possible competition.

Other considerations impacting the probability of successful competition assessment are an employee's age (are they more interested in retirement than competing) and health (are there any physical issues that would preclude competing).

Oftentimes the rock stars who are bound by a Non-Compete are also incentivized to remain with the company, either through compensation schemes, retained ownership in the company, or sometimes it's simply quality-of-life issues.

When considering all of these mitigating factors, the resulting probability of successful competition can be quite low. When that is the case, applying that low probability factor to the present value of the economic damages is an adjustment that will significantly reduce the  value of the economic damages, and thus result in a much lower value being ascribed to the Non-Compete, and by inference, the rock star.

There's More to the Story

What if a rock star leaves an organization and is not actually successful in competing? The factors we just looked at regarding the odds of success suggest that, in fact, the rock star will likely not become a successful competitor. However, that doesn't necessarily diminish the impact of their departure, as there are other considerations, like the loss of leadership and morale.

Additionally, what about the exceptional leaders – who may be difference makers and purple squirrels – who sit in various departments across the organization who are not bound by a Non-Compete or don't make a *direct* economic contribution? Once again, when determining value, these folks are often overlooked and their weighty contributions to the organization never hit the financial statements.

They might be the nurses in Pre-Op who move the patients through the process while allaying their fears and putting them at greater ease, or the teachers who stay late to  help their students, or that guy in the IT department who always saves the day when your computer freezes. Their titles might suggest that they are not members of the leadership team but they are leaders nonetheless. The ones with positive attitudes. The ones who build morale and help their teammates. The ones who inspire others to do great things.

You already know, without me telling you, that there is real value in those things and the people who possess those characteristics. It's a tough enough exercise to value the rock stars, so how can we possibly put a value on those in the organization who aren't perceived as such but who are making a positive difference every single day?

Chapter Seven:

Happiness or Success: Which Comes First?

"A little girl falls from her bunk bed and lands hard on the floor. She might have broken her leg, and she's in tremendous pain. As she is about to cry, her quick-thinking older brother tells her that no human could possibly have landed the way that she did when she hit the floor and that can only mean one thing: She's a unicorn.

"Rather than giving in to the pain, the little girl's brain begins to process the concept that she might actually be a baby unicorn."

This story of using positive psychology is shared by Shawn Achor, happiness researcher and noted for his advocacy of positive psychology, in his TED Talk, "The Happy Secret to Better Work," and is an example of how re-framing your circumstances can allow you to achieve a better / happier mindset.

Happiness, productivity, and success are all connected.

Are Successful People Happy? Are Happy People Successful?

You've probably heard people say that they "only hire the best and brightest"… from the best schools or with the best grades. So you may have been somewhat surprised to have learned in our discussion about Grit that intelligence is not a good predictor of success.

Here's more evidence on why intelligence alone is not a good predictor of success. In his TED Talk, Shawn Achor explains that his research reveals that an individual's success at work has less to do with intelligence and more to do with levels of optimism, social support, and the ability to see stress as a challenge.

Intuitively, we probably can relate firsthand that the opposite is true. For example, if we're experiencing unhappiness or distress, we're likely to be distracted and consequently less motivated and engaged at work. But while this negative side of the coin might be a relatable analogy, the positive side of that coin is also true.

The Disengaged Majority

According to Gallup, engaged employees are "involved in, enthusiastic about and committed to their work. Engaged employees support the innovation, growth and revenue that their companies need."

However, Gallup finds that most U.S. workers continue to fall into the not engaged category. These are not the ones we would classify as toxic employees (more on that in a subsequent chapter); rather these employees show up to kill time. Their efforts are essentially the bare minimum. As Gallup notes, "They are also more likely to miss work and change jobs when new opportunities arise."

Put simply, the way people feel at work profoundly influences how they perform.

According to the 2017 Gallup Survey, two-thirds (67 percent) of U.S. workers were not engaged in their jobs. Interestingly, while only 33 percent of employees were engaged at their jobs, this represents the highest level of engagement since Gallup started measuring such things. Worldwide, the level of employee engagement is even lower at 13 percent.

The Engaged Minority

So what about that engaged minority – the ones who I referred to as the rock stars, difference makers, and purple squirrels in earlier chapters? What value are these positive difference makers bringing to their organizations?

In a 2015 study entitled *The Relationship between Human Capital, Value Creation and Employee Reward* by Peter R. Massingham and Leona Tam of the University of

Wollongong in Australia, the researchers demonstrated a clear link to the impact of happiness on productivity.

While employees have various capabilities, it's how those capabilities are utilized that ultimately brings value to the organization.

According to the Australian research: "Employee capability may or may not generate value. It is only when individuals are motivated to use their knowledge that it creates organizational benefit; otherwise, it is an idle resource."

Employees who are happy at work and feel a sense of satisfaction about their jobs are more committed to their work and more motivated to work on important tasks. They are more likely to have positive attitudes regarding their jobs and they are more likely to utilize their capabilities that create value for their organization. This is an important finding that *confirms the importance of employee morale on productivity.*

Professors Andrew Oswald, Dr. Eugenio Proto, and Dr. Daniel Sgroi from the Department of Economics at the University of Warwick in the UK were able to quantify the impact of morale on productivity. According to their research, happiness made people around 12 percent more productive. Productivity was also demonstrated to increase by as much as 20 percent over shorter durations of concentrated work.

Shawn Achor refers to this link between happiness and productivity as "The Happiness Advantage," which indicates that the human brain performs significantly better in a happy state than it otherwise does in a neutral or negative state. The data that Shawn cites in his book of the same name demonstrates that "when we are positive, our brains become more engaged, creative, motivated, energetic, resilient, and productive at work." So, you may be surprised to learn that, according to Shawn's research: "Happiness fuels success, not the other way around."

The Happiness Advantage

In terms of the impact of happiness on productivity, Shawn's research is even more compelling than the other studies mentioned here. As he's noted: "Every single business and educational outcome improves when we start at positive rather than waiting for a future success. Sales improve 37 percent cross-industry, productivity by 31 percent, you're 40 percent more likely to receive a promotion, nearly ten times more engaged at work, live longer, get better grades, your symptoms are less acute, and much more."

> *Happiness is a huge driver of success, productivity, advancement, and health.*

Clearly, happiness has many more positive effects than just the propensity to be more successful at our jobs.

The health benefits are significant, and from a business perspective, a healthy employee costs less than an employee who is ill, in terms of insurance costs as well as downtime.

Shawn Achor says that happiness is a choice, so why not start there? If you'd like to choose happiness, Shawn has some tips for how you can rewire your brain and get to your happy place:

1. **Gratitude Exercises.** Write down three things you're grateful for that occurred over the last 24 hours. They don't have to be profound. It could be a really good cup of coffee or the warmth of a sunny day.

2. **The Doubler.** Take one positive experience from the past 24 hours and spend two minutes writing down every detail about that experience. As you remember it, your brain labels it as meaningful and deepens the imprint.

3. **The Fun Fifteen.** Do 15 minutes of a fun cardio activity, like gardening or walking the dog, every day. The effects of daily cardio can be as effective as taking an antidepressant.

4. **Meditation.** Every day take two minutes to stop whatever you're doing and concentrate on breathing. Even a short mindful break can result in a calmer, happier you.

5. **Conscious act of kindness.** At the start of every day, send a short email or text praising someone you know. Our brains become addicted to feeling good by making others feel good.

6. **Deepen Social Connections.** Spend time with family and friends. Our social connections are one of the best predictors for success and health, and even life expectancy.

Happiness or Success: Which Comes First?

Chapter Eight:

The Real Cost of Toxic Employees

With Candida Seasock and Michael Housman

Rock star employees make a huge positive impact and help to increase the valuation of the business. That's why finding a rock star is the goal of every hiring manager.

But is that really a good strategy?

Should organizations be focused on the positive (i.e., finding the rock stars)? Or are they better served trying to avoid the negative?

It's All about THEM

When we talk about toxic employees, we're talking about more than just a distracted employee who's perhaps spending some time at work on Facebook or a disengaged employee who's perhaps spending too much time at work on Careerbuilder looking for their next job. We're talking about the employees who are actively trying to get their colleagues to disengage, *or worse*.

Toxic employees don't care about a company's goals, nor do they care about building relationships with co-workers. More than just self-centered office bullies, toxic employees are actually strategic and covert.

A study by Michael Housman and Dylan Minor published in the *Harvard Gazette* defines a toxic employee as: "a worker that engages in behavior that is harmful to an organization, including either its property or people."

The data suggests that toxic employees drive other employees to leave an organization faster and more frequently, which generates huge turnover and training costs, and they diminish the productivity of everyone around them.

To gain some additional insights behind the research, I spoke with co-author, Dr. Michael Housman. According to Dr. Housman: "Behavior is contagious... we find that when a toxic person joins a team, others are more likely to behave in a toxic fashion."

Although not part of the Harvard study, Minor was quoted as saying that "client-customer surveys indicate that toxic workers 'absolutely' tend to damage a firm's customer service reputation, which has a long-term financial impact that can be difficult to quantify."

The Harvard study also estimated the value of finding a "rock star," defined as a worker in the top one percent of productivity, as compared to the value of avoiding a toxic worker.

According to the findings, by avoiding the hiring of a toxic employee, companies will save an average of $12,489 through the avoidance of potential litigation fees and avoiding a reduction in employee morale and productivity among other things.

The table below compares the cost savings associated with hiring a rock star compared to avoiding the hire of a toxic employee:

Rock Star Rank	Cost Savings	
	Hire a Rock Star	Avoid a Toxic Worker
Top 25%	$ 1,951	$12,489
Top 10%	$3,251	$12,489
Top 5%	$3,875	$12,489
Top 1%	$5,303	$12,489

The findings show that avoiding a toxic employee generates returns of nearly two-to-one as compared to those generated when firms hire a top one-percent rock star. This suggests more broadly that "bad" employees may have a stronger effect on the firm than "good" employees.

Skill versus Attitude

To further my understanding of the impact of toxic employees, I visited with Candida Seasock, founder of CTS & Associates. Candida has successfully assisted management teams ranging from Fortune 500 corporations to emerging growth companies through her award-winning approach "Growth Path to Success."

According to Candida, companies make the mistake  of hiring potentially toxic employees by not focusing on hiring to fit corporate culture. "Skills can be taught or developed, but honesty and integrity are found from within," she says.

Candida also warns that some of a company's earliest hires might not be the best fit as the company grows. "Holding on to employees who are resistant to change and growth can result in toxic behaviors as those employees try to survive," she says.

This can be a costly mistake.

According to this article by Jeremy Goldman in *Inc,*. "Here's How Much Your Bad Employees Are Costing You," the cost of keeping the wrong person can be up to 15 times their annual salary. The impact to the company includes the following:

1) Losing great employees who quit because they don't want to work with a toxic employee anymore;

2) Customers/clients won't work with you because of their experience with the toxic employee; and

3) New potential rock star employees won't join the company because they've heard bad things about the company's culture. (Recall from an earlier chapter that in this age of transparency, it's easy for these folks to research the organization.)

The fact that toxic employees are costly to the firms that employ them isn't really much of a shocker, but there is a little bit of irony that is derived from the research. Specifically, the Harvard study also found that: **Toxic employees are much more productive than the average employee.** This helps to explain how superstar athletes who are bad in the locker room or have off-the-field issues, for example, can remain with their teams.

Dr. Housman notes, however, that "while toxic employees are more productive, meaning getting more things done, the quality of that productivity often is less than desirable."

The challenge: Toxic employees might also be productive employees.

Organizations are often confronted with the situation in which they need to decide whether to terminate a high-performing toxic employee for the betterment of the team's morale. How many are able to do that, as compared to looking the other way because the employee's "numbers were just too good"?

Candida says that "the toxic employees are top performers because they've literally become know-it-alls. As a result of their behaviors, they pick up valuable pieces of information along the way."

But these behaviors can only be tolerated up to a certain point.

Productivity or Toxicity

Presented with the apparent correlation of high productivity among the toxic employees, the Harvard researchers explicitly examined the trade-off in increased productivity versus the propensity for toxicity.

As it turns out, *avoiding* toxic workers is still better for the organization in terms of net profitability, despite losing out on a highly productive employee.

Avoiding a toxic employee (or coaching them up to an average employee) enhances performance to a much greater extent than replacing an average employee with a rock star.

What role does management play in creating or fostering a toxic environment? According to Dr. Housman, even when management teams are not contributing to the toxic behaviors, he says that: "*By not* policing toxic behaviors, management can create an environment where people feel that they can 'get away with' behaving badly."

Clearly it's best to avoid hiring a toxic employee in the first place, but if you've got them in your midst, Candida recommends that the toxic employee either needs to be terminated or isolated. For management teams that just can't give up the high performance, Candida emphasizes the need to "recognize the toxic behavior and separate the toxic employee from the rest of the workforce by letting them focus on what they're really good at."

But at some point, the toxic behavior outweighs the high performance.

Afraid to cut the cord? Wondering if removing a toxic superstar really pays dividends? Consider the real world example of a Philadelphia-area precision metal shop. A good worker with a bully-ish attitude forced the owner to re-think his company culture and values. Despite trying to coach the toxic employee on behavior, nothing stuck. He finally offered a generous severance and let him go along with two others. This company closely monitored productivity in sales shipped per direct labor hour. With the toxic employee in place, that statistic was in the $85 to $90/hour range. A month after he was let go, it rose to $123/hour. Another telling statistic: Productivity had the greatest increase in the departments that operated in close proximity to the toxic employee. (See the Resource section for the link to the entire story.)

So is letting a toxic employee go the best solution, or can a toxic employee really be rehabilitated? Can their attitudes be changed and perspectives be altered so that toxic employees can move up to average? In the next chapter, we'll discuss the impact of attitude and perspective.

Chapter Nine:

The Impact of Attitude and Perspective

With Bev Borton and Dave Nast

Is the glass half-full, or is the glass half-empty?

Is the glass is really twice the size it needs to be?

 Or does it even matter because the glass can always be re-filled?

The way you think about the answer to this age-old question is reflective of your perspective.

In short, your perspectives are a function of your experiences and are at the center of understanding how you behave and how you lead.

When thinking about the value of people, the "intangibles within the intangible," like attitude, perspective, and mindset, are especially difficult to quantify. While a valuation of a business is always as of a particular point in time, when we think about people, it's possible to think about that snapshot of value as really being representative of a *potential value* at any point in time.

For example... photograph a child. That image captures a moment – one particular moment in time, but what can it predict about the future? Will she be happy in her relationships? Will she be a good parent? Will future circumstances lead her up the scale or down the scale of opportunities? In essence, her success and happiness in life will be based on her capacity to tap her potential, use her influence, and navigate change. The same is true of our organizations as it is the workforce that represents the true potential of any business.

An Organization Is a Living Organism

When you think about an organization as a living and dynamic thing, patterns begin to emerge. Just as in nature, for example, the business world is also ordered by patterns. While some patterns are obvious, there are patterns regarding attitudes, decision making, performance, and priorities that we often ignore. Like the growing child in the photograph we snapped, our patterns of leadership behavior affect our potential, our influence, and our ability to adapt to change.

These behavioral patterns are often a direct result of perspective.

To get a better sense on how perspective impacts behavior and performance, I met up with Beverly Borton, founder of Bev Borton Coaching. Bev is certified in Energy Leadership and has devoted her career to helping people understand that small shifts in our perceptions can open us up to a world of possibilities that we didn't know existed.

Bev says: "Organizations are simply people in relationship with a similar purpose or goal. People are behind every assessment and measurement that one can perform pertaining to a business. People create the processes and perform the work; people make decisions and people do the communicating."

Perspective in Action

Think about a football coach who played a defensive position during their playing career. Defense was their priority and their passion. It's what they know best.

When elevated to the role of head coach, their perspective may carry such an emphasis on defense that it eclipses the importance of developing a solid offense.

Their teams are assembled based upon their biases (perspectives), and the resulting behaviors of the members of the teams have often limited their ability to be successful.

It's the same in the business world.

Frequent collaborator in this book (and online series), Dave Nast of Nast Partners is a Certified Workplace Behavior Analyst and has met with hundreds of business owners. When he asks a CEO to rate their team on a scale of one to ten, he most often hears five or six as the answer.

With that in mind, if Dave comes in to coach and train their team with a focus on improving their skills and knowledge, he might raise that team up to a six or seven. But, he says, "If I want to close that gap, I need to coach and train them on their attitude and perspective."

In the case of the football coach, his perspective was always from the viewpoint of the defense, ultimately struggling to have a winning team, so let's consider another example of how a broader perspective can, in fact, create positive results. Attorney Nella Bloom authored a post "Monet and Manufacturing – Painting a Picture of Employee Satisfaction," based on her experience as a research assistant in a paint manufacturing plant. She came to realize that everyone working in the factory, from the CEO to workers on the factory floor, shared the same perspective: They weren't making paint. They were making art. From their points of view, "making paint was making art, and art changes the world." That shared, broad perspective created satisfaction at every level and subsequently created very positive results.

> *We are all driven by or limited by our own perspectives.*

Perspectives Become Behaviors

I was familiar with personality-based assessments, such as Myers Briggs; however, I had not heard of an assessment offered by the Institute for Professional Excellence in Coaching (iPEC) – iPEC's Energy Leadership Index (E.L.I.).

This is an attitudinal assessment that is based on an energy/action model. The assessment differs from personality assessments in that it is not intended to label a person and have them work well within that label. Instead, it measures a level of energy based on a person's attitude and perspective of their world.

> *Keep your thoughts positive because your thoughts become your words.*
> *Keep your words positive because your words become your behavior.*
> *Keep your behavior positive because your behavior becomes your habits.*
> *Keep your habits positive because your habits become your values.*
> *Keep your values positive because your values become your destiny.*
> *~Mahatma Gandhi*

It's the thoughts that give rise to emotions that cause us to act in certain ways. This chain forms our perceptions or attitudes and explains why we can expose a roomful of people to the same event and later elicit differing interpretations of what occurred.

However, because attitude is subjective, it can be altered and, with that, change one's perspective and behaviors.

Energy Leadership

Energy Leadership is a process that develops a personally effective style of leadership that positively influences not only one's self but also those with whom they interact. Energy Leadership traits include, among other things, emotional intelligence and leadership effectiveness.

An Average Resonating Level of Energy, or "E-Factor," from this assessment reflects an individual's overall satisfaction in life and at work. Those with higher E-Factors are very satisfied with their relationships, the level of engagement at work, and their level of leadership and communication skills. Those with lower E-Factors work to raise them, but it all starts with an awareness of where they are.

Once people become aware of their attitudes and motivations, they can shift their energy and focus in a transformational way. For example, this attitudinal awareness can move someone from a perspective of scarcity (i.e., "What's in it for me?") to a perspective of abundance (i.e., "How do we all benefit?") As you can imagine, there is a great difference in the decision-making and leadership effectiveness between individuals on either end of that spectrum.

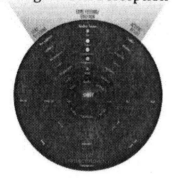

Energetic Self Perception

© Bruce D. Schneider 2006

In a previous chapter, we discussed the real cost of toxic employees and the value that can be created by coaching a toxic employee up to average. I asked Bev for her perspective on rehabilitating a toxic employee. Not surprisingly, Bev believes that it is possible to address the energy behind his or her thinking.

Bev says that an effective leader at E-Factor Level 5 or 6 will act in ways that can help to shift the perspectives of people at Level 2, for example, by handling their issues differently and giving them opportunities to rise to Level 3 or higher. But she adds: "While employees with destructive energy can be elevated to constructive levels, it will take a committed effort from all parties."

Dave Nast adds that you can increase engagement in the workplace by taking the time to understand the perspectives of your employees. He says: "When needs are met at work, performance, productivity, and engagement go up (along with ROI)."

The Impact of Attitude and Perspective

Chapter Ten:

The Secret to Innovation: Trust

With Art Dimitri and Monique Caissie

When you think of the concept of innovation, it usually brings to mind major shifts in technology, like the introduction of a new smart phone. Or in science, the introduction of a new drug. Or perhaps in cuisine, chocolate-dipped bacon. (That might just be one of the best uses for chocolate since its marriage with peanut butter.)

But innovation is often born from small things, and it requires a fundamental element to exist within an organization's culture. That's trust.

Where Do the Good Ideas Come From?

Not all innovation represents a seismic shift from the status quo. Sometimes very small tweaks to a process can result in time savings or quality improvements. And who better to get such ideas from than the people in the trenches who would know best?

Perhaps one of the more critical elements for good teamwork is trust. When trust goes up, fear goes down and vice versa. When people work or play well together, it means that there is high trust in the group, and trust leads to innovation.

Meet Art Dimitri, an expert on innovation. Art believes that the best ideas come from a company's employees. Unfortunately, many great ideas never see the light of day. Why is that?

Art spent his career being responsible for driving innovation at various firms. Innovation is also somewhat of a hobby for him – it's just who he is. Wherever he goes, Art keenly observes employee interactions, and he likes to ask the employees questions like, "What would you do if you had a great idea that would really improve the way things are run? Is there a process for that and would you be comfortable doing it?"

I've been in Art's company when he's done this and observed firsthand some of the responses. Some employees said that management doesn't seem to welcome ideas – they're certainly not requested. Some employees said that they would likely share the idea with their immediate supervisor, but they didn't know what any next steps were after that or if they should expect any kind of feedback. Some employees just didn't think it was worth the effort.

But why not?

Who Exactly Is Taking the Risk?

As an organization, you want your people to be engaged and comfortable to submit their ideas. Don't you?

For an employee to think about idea generation, they're going to assume a fair amount of risk. Risk that they might be ridiculed for making a silly suggestion or risk that they might not be rewarded if their idea leads to something great. Or even the risk of working on a project that fails could be damaging to their career.

Art shares a story about a supermarket produce manager with more than 25 years of experience. Two months earlier, his former employer was acquired by another supermarket chain. When Art asked how interested the new management team was in his ideas for best practices in displaying fruits and vegetables, he said, "They weren't." No one asked him anything, but they were very quick to teach him their way. He felt the message was clear. *Their way was the right way.*

Art puts it this way, "An employee's fear of failure destroys the trust to experiment that is required for innovation."

The Business Case for Trust

Great Place to Work (GPTW) is a leading authority on building and recognizing high-trust, high-performing workplace cultures. Their 30 years of research in numerous countries around the world has shown repeatedly that investing in a high-trust workplace culture yields tangible business benefits.

GPTW has found that employees experience high levels of trust in the workplace when they:

1. Believe leaders are credible (i.e., competent, communicative, honest).
2. Believe they are treated with respect as people and professionals.
3. Believe the workplace is fundamentally fair.

The GPTW annual studies of the *Fortune 100 Best Companies to Work For* show that great workplaces enjoy **almost three times better cumulative financial performance** than their industry peers. Those companies also experience improvements on higher customer satisfaction, improved employee morale, safety, higher quality job applicants, and **innovation**. Annualized returns for high-trust-culture companies also exceed the overall market.

Luigi Guiso, of the Einaudi Institute for Economics and Finance, led a study of roughly 700 companies that completed the Great Place to Work Trust Index Survey. The result was that in those companies where employees reported that their leaders act with integrity (key to building trust), a number of competitive advantages emerged, including: **higher productivity, increased profitability,** and **greater attraction of top job applicants.**

Another study performed by German consultancy IZA, a private independent economic research institute focused on the analysis of global labor markets, corroborates these findings as well.

The data prove that trust is good for business.

Still need more evidence? Check out the findings in the article, "Neuroscience of Trust" by Dr. Paul J. Zak, which also finds that there is a return-on-trust: "Compared with people at low-trust companies, people at high-trust companies report: 74% less stress, 106% more energy at work, 50% higher productivity, 13% fewer sick days, 76% more engagement, 29% more satisfaction with their lives, 40% less burnout."

The Human Case for Trust

Social media allows us to have a lot of connections – many of them likely being superficial at best. But we humans still desire a genuine connection. We want to have real relationships with real people and organizations that we trust. As much of innovation these days involves collaboration, trust among fellow employees as well as between the employee and employer is critical.

If an organization wants to encourage their people to take the risk of innovation, they need to have the necessary thick skin to receive criticisms that are the starting point of idea generation. It's not enough for the organization to simply say the words; employees need to trust that the words are sincere and that

"If you don't have a culture where people feel that it's OK to take a risk, with the understanding that the risk could fail, you're unlikely to have much innovation, and a willingness to take on risk is all about trust." ~ *Alan Webber, Co-Founding Editor, Fast Company, USA*

they can take such risks without repercussion.

Trust in the workplace starts at the top of the organizational chart and at the top of each department. It needs to be woven into the fabric of the corporate culture. And it all begins and ends with the **people**.

Author and speaker, Brené Brown, discusses "The Anatomy of Trust" in her appearance on *SuperSoul.TV*. She notes that, among other things, trust is built in what she refers to as the small moments. Those seemingly insignificant acts like asking how someone's sick child is doing. That's called empathy, and it builds trust.

> *"My experience is that significant distrust doubles the cost of doing business and triples the time it takes to get things done."*
> ~ *Steven Covey*

According to Steven Covey, author of *The Speed of Trust: The One Thing That Changes Everything*: "When trust is low, in a company or in a relationship, it places a hidden 'tax' on every transaction: every communication, every interaction, every strategy, every decision is taxed, bringing speed down and sending costs up."

Speaker and consultant, Monique Caissie notes that even in mature teams that are used to working together, trust can suffer by adding a newcomer to the team or by modifying a goal. In her article, "How Leaders Can Improve Teamwork and Build Trust," Monique outlines five key things that good leaders will do to introduce trust-building actions to the team:

1. **Choose to believe and trust.** This is where great leaders take their first steps intelligently and with integrity. They choose to believe and trust in the process and in the people they work with.
2. **Start with themselves.** They make sure they are themselves competent to their jobs and trustworthy to others who count on them.
3. **Declare their intents and assume positive intent in others.** Trusting leaders openly express their commitment to trusting others and their expectations that others should be trustworthy.
4. **Do what they say they are going to do.** These smart leaders can easily follow through on their promises because they only state what they know they can follow through on.
5. **Lead out in extending trust to others.** Modeling their expectations, they are the first to believe others. They give them chances where others have doubted them. This fosters good feelings and increases trust.

Monique states, "When fear is predominant, we convince ourselves that we should wait until others prove themselves to us. That only serves to create suspicion and more fear."

Monique believes that while the trust theories are so logical, they can be difficult to implement because trust-based leadership is not natural for everyone. Healthy human relation habits can be hard and can feel risky to adopt when trust is currently low, but a smart leader knows that someone needs to trust first, and it starts with them.

The Secret to Innovation: Trust

Chapter Eleven:

How to Destroy Trust

With Stephan Seyfert

While we're on the topic of building trust, it might be worthwhile to understand how easy it is to lose trust.

In the book, the *Go-Giver* by Bob Burg and John David Mann, they make the case that, "all things being equal, people are more likely to do business with, and refer business to, people that they know, like and trust."

Know. Like. Trust.

The "know" part is relatively easy.

The "like" part, while a little more challenging, is still relatively easy as long as you're not a jerk.

The "trust" part is hard. Building trust takes time.

But destroying trust can happen in the blink of an eye.

For this topic, I visited with internationally sought-after business advisor, Stephan Seyfert.

Shortly after receiving one of Stephan's first awards in the Navy, his supervisor pulled him aside.

"Congratulations," he started, smiling. "I expect this is the first of many 'atta-boys' you'll receive in your career."

Then he quietly said something that stuck with Stephan and which he's shared with others for more than 25 years.

"Just remember," he said, "One 'oops' erases a thousand 'atta-boys'."

That wisdom has proven to be true, time and time again. Whether in sales or leadership, guiding individuals or leading teams and creating cultures, Stephan has learned how important it is to establish, maintain, and continually nurture and grow rapport. "Rapport is critical, and its core is trust," he says.

Just like every accolade earned becomes a deposit in the bank, every moment of building trust is stored up. When we mess up – when we have an "oops" moment – we need to have enough stored up in that bank to offset the damage done. While not scientific, Stephan believes that it's about a 1,000:1 ratio... just as his Navy supervisor suggested.

It's no different with any other relationships. Whether in business, at home, or in our communities, we have to continually work to deposit those coins in our "trust bank," so we have them available when needed.

How Do We Destroy Trust?

It might seem like we're simply looking at the other side of the same coin of building trust, and that's partially true. Obviously, to break trust, you do the opposite of what you do to build trust. Sometimes you don't even need to do a thing. Sometimes it's just the **fear** that you might go against your word that causes distrust. That kind of fear likely stems from how the other person has been treated previously and is known  as having trust-issues, but that discussion is way beyond the scope of this discussion.

However, there is a different type of fear that bubbles up in organizations. This fear stems from a corporate culture that lacks clear, consistent communication and from behaviors that are consistent with such communication.

So if building trust is a by-product of intention – the result of living with character and integrity – then breaking trust, therefore, is a by-product of carelessness, lack of focus, and inattention.

It's what happens when we don't keep a watchful eye on ourselves and don't allow others to be empowered to speak truth to us. As Stephan says, "It's what happens when we think of ourselves as soloists, independent of the orchestra or even blessing them by the music we play to them."

Having worked in small organizations and large bureaucracies, Stephan has observed that the absence of trust – or fear – is often the key limiting factor to how successful an organization can become.

When a bureaucracy as large as the U.S. government gets it, you can be sure that it matters.

In the exhaustive manual, *Maximizing Employee Engagement – Participant Guide,* the United States Office of Personnel Management (OPM) Executive Services Department included a Job Aid section entitled *"Fast Track to Lowering Engagement"* in which they list the quickest ways to lower employee engagement. We've added a few of our own to their list, and all of these speak to issues of trust:

- Emotionally ignorant managers
- Failing to include employee engagement as a performance metric in managers' performance plans
- Failing to tailor engagement efforts to the culture/climate of your agency
- Failing to appropriately reward or promote employees
- Too many management layers
- Failing to provide transparent and trustworthy senior leadership
- Failing to provide the right tools and resources for employees to effectively do their jobs
- Failing to communicate a clear vision of the agency's mission
- Secrecy around (bad) news
- Failing to communicate openly, frequently, and effectively with employees about organizational challenges, as well as organizational achievements

- Failure to have open two-way communication with the workforce, to include communicating with employees as a group and on an individual basis
- Failure to value the individual
- Failing to include and solicit feedback from employees in developing strategies and recommendations for agency improvements
- Failing to have senior leaders take an active interest in Employee Viewpoint Survey results and develop agency-wide and office plans for improvements
- Failing to empower employees to be innovative and find ways to better perform their jobs
- Failing to help employees see line-of-sight between their work and the agency's mission
- Failing to recognize and acknowledge good work
- Failing to provide opportunities for career advancement and provide greater responsibilities or new experiences
- Failing to incorporate team problem solving and decision making, especially where it affects them

The OPM guide wisely states the way to help create a culture of engagement is to "create a sense of trust and transparency with leadership."

Stephan says that he would go a step further and say to not just create a sense, "but to create **actual** trust and transparency with leadership. Be intentional about it. Monitor it. Measure it. Expect it. Demand it. It's too important not to do so."

The OPM offers three specific actions to build trust and increase engagement, which will probably sound familiar:

- Communicate a clear vision of how the agency will accomplish its mission
- Communicate honestly about the organization and ensure that your words are consistent with your actions
- Ensure there is transparency between decisions and the strategic direction of the organization

That sounds like a good way to conduct business, coach a team, lead a family, or simply to live life. After all, success in any meaningful endeavor requires the collaboration of more than one individual, each shining in his or her role. Success in leadership, sales, and developing other people (as individuals and in teams and cultures) rests entirely on building and maintaining rapport – and trust is the central component of rapport.

Small Things Matter

We must also remember that trust isn't only important in the big moments. In fact, it happens every day in the small moments that, together, are far more important than the big ones.

Author and speaker Brené Brown, an expert on the importance of transparency and vulnerability to establishing and growing trust, notes that trust can be lost in the small moments such as missing an opportunity to connect with an individual as an individual by showing genuine curiosity, care, and interest. Choosing not to connect with someone that way is essentially an act of betrayal that will destroy trust. It's that little "oops" that wipes out the "atta-boys." Conversely, every time you intentionally connect in a small meaningful way, it's like dropping another coin in that "bank of trust."

As Stephan notes: "The key is to be genuine about it. You can't fake it. Most people have highly calibrated 'BS' detectors, and they are always on alert. The first sign of insincerity will end it."

My "BS" detector has fresh batteries, too.

We might summarize it down to the classic Golden Rule: Treat others as you wish to be treated. Trust, after all, is a two-way street. You must give it in order to receive it.

How to Destroy Trust

Chapter Twelve:

Do You Believe in Miracles? Why Some Teams Succeed While Others Fail

With Dr. Janice Presser

"Do you believe in miracles?"

Those words, uttered in the final seconds of the game, memorialized the great and improbable victory by the U.S. hockey team over the Soviet Union during the 1980 Olympics.

It is a great story of a group of underdogs pulling together as a team that it was dubbed the "Miracle On Ice," and it was made into a movie that was simply titled *Miracle*.

What is it about certain teams that allow the individuals to rise above their own abilities to achieve results that they could never otherwise accomplish?

The Team Is a Group of Individuals

There is no "I" in team. Or is there?

Teams are comprised of a group of Individuals (capital "I"). Why is it that the teams with the best individual athletes don't always deliver the championships?

Sports, be it at the pee-wee level through the highly paid professional levels, provides the opportunity for a group of individuals to come together in pursuit of a common goal. Is it this higher pursuit and the understanding that it can only be achieved if everyone pulls together the magic behind team building?

When we think about measuring employees by the numbers, the world of sports makes it easy for benchmark comparisons. There are certainly plenty of superstar athletes whose statistics far exceed their peers, so they're paid accordingly. But why, then, are these superior performers often the biggest problems for their teams rather than the keys to winning championships? To use an expression that we've already discussed, these are the high-performing but toxic employees.

If you think about it, a sports team is essentially an assembled workforce with some particularly unique talents. When we think about an assembled workforce in the business context, we generally don't think about it in terms of its ability to perform in life-and-death situations. But let's go there for just a moment.

Think about the interactions of a medical team in the emergency room. How those teams work together can literally be the difference between life and death for the patient. And in some occupations, the interactions of the

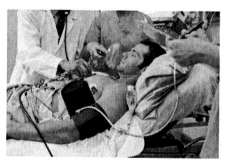

team can difference between life and death for *themselves*. It's true when you think about an organization as the metaphorical patient in this scenario. And it's also true when thinking about the chemistry of the sports teams that fail to live up to expectations. There is a common thread in all of this.

The Team Is More than the Sum of the Parts

At some point in your career, you might have been required to take a personality test, an aptitude test, or maybe even an intelligence test. Identifying these traits are useful tools, but unfortunately, hiring the best and brightest individuals doesn't guarantee having the best team. This begs the question: What is Teaming, can it be measured, and if so, how might that information improve the world of work?

To get the answer, I visited with Dr. Janice Presser, co-founder and Chief Executive Officer of the Gabriel Institute. Dr. Presser has dedicated her career to answering that question. She is a behavioral

> *"It's better to have a great team than a team of greats."*
> *~ Simon Sinek*

scientist and the architect of the technology that powers Teamability®. She has devoted most of her working life to the study of team interaction in its many forms and is an authority in the measurement of individual and group teaming behaviors.

"A group of people become a team when they have a common goal. Great teaming happens when people team well with each other, and also with the mission of the team," states Dr. Presser.

Teamability is the result of 25 years of behavioral science research and technology development. It combines technology with integrated team analysis and management methods based on fundamental differences in the way people seek to make meaningful team contributions.

Teamability was engineered to provide leadership guidance, to improve workplace engagement, and to sustain organizational health and productivity. And as I like to point out, these things all tend to increase the valuation of the business enterprise.

Who's on the Bus and Where Do They Sit?

While tests for personality, aptitudes, interests, and values are designed to measure what's going on inside of a person, Teamability was engineered to measure what is actually happening when people team together to achieve a common goal.

An article that discussed Google's work on effective teams found that "it has less to do with who is on a team and more with how a team's members interact with one another." This might run somewhat counter to what you've previously been told about this topic. For example, in his book *Good to Great*, Jim Collins talks about the importance of "having the right people on the bus, and having the right people in the right seat on the bus." A skeptic might also suggest that a company like Google will always attract the best talent, so the "who" part of the equation is a given. Having spent as much time as I have with Dr. Presser in learning about teaming, I believe that the importance of having the right person in the right job with the right responsibilities should not be underestimated.

Know Your Role

In the world of Teamability, a person's Role is not a job title, or list of job responsibilities. Rather, someone's Role is a highly reliable indicator of the kind of contributions a person will want to do and will enjoy doing for the long haul.

This helps us understand why the company's top salesperson struggles with (read: hates) doing administrative tasks like expense reports and conversely, why the company's top technical analyst struggles with being on a sales call.

Taking this a step further, every role has a complementary role partner. This is key to building high quality into the team structure. Not all teams require all of the roles, and role partners need not always be on the same team.

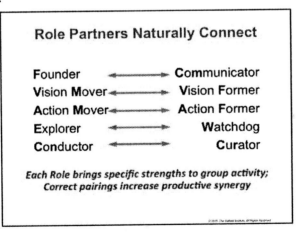

```
Role Partners Naturally Connect

Founder          ◄──────►  Communicator
Vision Mover ◄──────►  Vision Former
Action Mover ◄──────►  Action Former
Explorer         ◄──────►  Watchdog
Conductor        ◄──────►  Curator

Each Role brings specific strengths to group activity;
Correct pairings increase productive synergy
```

"How you team with your direct reports influences how they team with their direct reports, and so on down the line. Are you driving the culture that you say you want?" - Dr. Janice Presser

To continue with the sports analogy, the quarterback of a football team's role partner won't necessarily be his receivers. In fact, it may not even be anyone on the offense. The role partner could be one of the trainers, who helps the quarterback with physical therapy or a coach sitting in the press box with a bird's eye view of the field.

On every team, people must find ways to serve each other's needs. At the same time, each person has another relationship going on between themselves and the team itself. Both of these relationships are essential for the creation and maintenance of positive team chemistry. (In the spirit of transparency, according to Teamability, I am an "Action Mover.")

According to Dr. Presser, "If you don't start by understanding your mission – which should be driven by your long-range vision – you won't know what you are quantifying against. Once you know that, do you have people who meet the needs of that mission? And are you getting the synergies that would enhance every person's baseline value?"

It's not enough to just have a group of outstanding individual employees. Inevitably, people will need to work together, and their ability to function as a team is perhaps even more critical than the individuals who comprise the team.

> *"Do not tolerate brilliant jerks. The cost to teamwork is too high."*
> *~ Reed Hastings, CEO, Netflix*

As Dr. Presser says: "It always goes back to the needs of the team. Those who serve above and beyond will impact your bottom line, directly or indirectly."

Back to the Ice

It's important to remember that being a part of a team is more than just wearing the same uniform or having the same logo on your ID badge.

Teaming is about getting the various Individuals (capital "I") to rally behind a common goal (and each other) and fostering a culture of collaboration that drives performance.

Goaltender for that U.S. hockey team, Jim Craig, said, "Coach Herb Brooks wasn't coaching a 'Dream Team' – he was coaching a team of Dreamers."

Herb Brooks emphasized that the name on the front of the jersey (the team name) mattered more than the name on the back of the jersey (the player's name). He sought out players who believed what he believed, and together, they accomplished the unthinkable.

"When you pull on that jersey, you represent yourself and your teammates, and the name on the front is a hell of a lot more important than the one on the back. Get that through your head!"
~ Herb Brooks

Chapter Thirteen:

What Flavor Is Your Kool-Aid?

With Al Cini

"They drank the Kool-Aid." That is a fairly common expression that is used in business and politics. The origin of the expression is often traced back to a tragic event in the late 1970s involving a cult's mass murder-suicide with poisoned Kool-Aid®. The phrase has since become colloquial for "someone who totally embraces an ideology or arguments."

Great companies all have employees who seem to be "drinking the same Kool-Aid." When you think about employees of Apple or Google, for example, you immediately get it. You can almost imagine a great leader serving up the company's Kool-Aid and offering the employees a glass. But how do those leaders decide what "flavor" of Kool-Aid to serve, and more importantly, how do they get everyone to drink it?

To understand this phenomenon, I sat down with Al Cini, President of Al Cini and Partners. Al is the inventor of the Brand and Culture Alignment Toolkit.

The Alignment of Brand and Culture

The Brand and Culture Alignment Toolkit (BCAT) is all about shifting people from merely "doing things" to actually getting things done.

Al says: "Something amazing happens whenever people willingly collaborate on accomplishing something together."

As people subordinate their individual egos to the collective pursuit of the mission they share, they adopt a common set of beliefs and values and begin to express them with similar language and observable patterns of behavior.

Their Culture is the set of beliefs and values they share, and their Brand is the collective pattern of language, traditions, and methods they use in their work.

An organization can be any size, from a couple of people on a small project team to thousands in a large corporation. The "Kool-Aid Effect" happens when they're all on the same page with each other, walking their talk, singing from the same hymnal.

Al refers to this phenomenon as the alignment of Brand (Behavior) with Culture (Beliefs), and he uses Kool-Aid as a simple learning metaphor for the established behavioral science behind it.

What "Flavors" Are Available?

 Imagine an organization's Brand and Culture as a blend of flavors in their water cooler. When people gather around the water cooler and drink from it together, they're savoring their Culture.

When they pour it out and serve it to their customers and stakeholders, they're expressing their Brand.

BCAT consists of instruments that, for any given group, team, or company, measure and quantify its signature Brand and Culture as a recipe combining four distinct "flavors."

Blue (Precision): People who enjoy this flavor share an affinity for research, meticulous investigation, objective measurement, and analytics. Organizations can add this flavor into their "water cooler" to encourage their members to become more deliberate, scientific, and objective in their work, and to communicate to the world at large that the organization values careful analysis and thorough consideration, and offers well-researched solutions.

Red (Purpose): Decisive people tend to enjoy this flavor – people who prefer simple arguments and clear action items. Organizations use this flavor to promote reliable, on-time delivery, and to communicate that they're known for assertively and competitively moving the ball forward and racking up clear victories.

Yellow (Innovation): Artists and explorers like this flavor – people who question the status quo and imagine a better future. Companies serve up this flavor to promote breakthrough, outside-the-box thinking, and to express that they're all about developing new ideas and delivering novel, creative solutions.

Green (Harmony): Green is the flavor preferred by people who respect and follow established tradition and value a strong community based on fair treatment for everyone. Green-serving organizations enjoy a reputation for due diligence, consistent performance, and taking good care of the people they serve.

These colors are based on the same well-established principles found in individual assessments like DISC and

Myers & Briggs. BCAT's four "flavors" represent the four patterns of collective thought and behavior exhibited by effective, mission-focused groups.

The BCAT model arranges these flavors into a four-quadrant Brand and Culture map that, as suggested by recent research, are reflected in four measurable patterns of brain activity.

They aren't always conscious of this, but, based on their common mission, all effective organizations mix the four flavors into their Brand and Culture water coolers.

Choose Your Flavor

The first step in Al's process in the BCAT Survey is designed to make an organization's leaders consciously aware of the signature water cooler recipe that makes them the very best at what they do.

The BCAT Survey is taken online, typically in less than 20 minutes. Participants are instructed to take a moment to visualize their group, team, company, or organization as though it were a person at work, using certain attributes and skills, doing its best to deliver on its

 mission and achieve its goals. With a visualization of this "virtual person" in mind, the BCAT Survey will profile this collective "Role Model," producing a report that characterizes the organization's Brand and Culture.

Getting People to Drink

While people will fight imposed change, they'll voluntarily change and improve themselves when given the proper encouragement and guidance. MIT professor and author, Peter Senge, put it this way: "People don't resist change. They resist being changed."

Research shows that people learn and improve by emulating role models.

BCAT's goal is to capture and communicate a pattern of ideal mission-aligned behavior that people at all levels of an organization can use to become better at work.

The ROI of Drinking the Kool-Aid

Of course, ROI (as in "Return on Individuals") is always the big question and the toughest to tackle.

Over a two-year period from 2013-2015, Al and his team collected and analyzed data from 620 participants in more than 60 groups, departments, and teams within 13 different commercial and nonprofit organizations, including media, manufacturing, and service delivery.

The results demonstrate that following the BCAT model improves employee engagement from 32 to 66 percent as benchmarked against Gallup's Q12 Employee Engagement Questionnaire.

In practical terms, Gallup's extensive research on the subject or employee engagement correlated the improved Q12 scores achieved by using BCAT, with the following measurable outcomes:

- Absenteeism: 37% lower

- Employee Turnover: 25% reduction in high-turnover organizations; 65% in low-turnover organizations
- Shrinkage: reduced by 28%
- Safety Incidents: 48% overall reduction; 41% reduction in health care patient safety
- Quality: 41% fewer defects
- Customer Satisfaction: 10% higher
- Employee Productivity: 21% higher
- Profitability: 22% higher

What's in Your Cooler?

Al tells me that he regularly works with client companies whose management can't agree on what flavor is, or even should be, in the water cooler.

Delivering the correct "Corporate Kool-Aid" begins with the leadership team being in complete alignment on what flavor is being served in the water cooler. Otherwise, there will likely be various flavors being served based upon the preferences of the individuals of a particular department, for example.

Al tells me that: "The key to achieving the psychological buy-in that turns a bunch of different people into a cohesive, effective team, is the clear understanding of what's in that water cooler."

When leaders take the time to mindfully express the core values (the Kool-Aid flavor recipe) that best embody the shared goals of the group, employees can pattern their individual behavior after this virtual role model and "drink the Kool-Aid" to become a more effective workforce.

Chapter Fourteen:

A Case of Corporate Cultures

With Andy Levin

While we've covered a lot of theory about corporate culture, I believe it's time to move out of the "text book and into the lab" by looking at two real world examples: Bai Brands and Material Handling Supply, Inc.

Bai Brands

You may be familiar with the antioxidant drink, Bai. As soon as you walk into its corporate offices, you know immediately that this company is different. It's more than the hip décor, the gastro-pub, or the coffee bar. The place has an energetic vibe about it that goes much deeper.

From its humble beginnings in 2008 in founder Ben Weiss's basement to its February 2017 acquisition by Dr. Pepper Snapple Group for $1.7 billion, Bai is a case study in how the people of an organization play a critical role in the valuation of that organization.

Some might describe Bai as a manufacturer of low calorie, antioxidant-infused beverages. But they'd be missing the point with that over-simplification. I had the pleasure of calling Bai a client and had the opportunity to visit with the company's founder and (now former) CEO, Ben Weiss about what's really behind the success of Bai.

Everyone at Bai is committed to a "bev-olution" that challenges the status quo, where doing what's right doesn't mean sacrificing enjoyment in a world where flavor and natural goodness go hand in hand. ***That's*** exactly the kind of message that gets people inspired to come to work!

Ben Weiss's journey began when he unearthed a secret kept by Indonesian coffee farmers: the antioxidant-

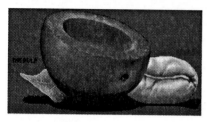

containing coffeefruit, once just a discarded by-product, had untapped potential to be included in a healthful drink. The coffee bean is actually the center of the coffeefruit. The coffeefruit's red pulp has free-radical-fighting antioxidants that help maintain the body's natural protection against potentially damaging processes such as oxidation.

The word "Bai" is a Mandarin word for "pure." It's also an acronym for "botanical antioxidant infusions."

Bai's Civet Society

Admittedly, Bai's Civit Society is a cultural driver in the company, but to fully appreciate its impact, you have to first understand the role of a civit in coffee production.

The civit is a small

mammal that lives in the trees on the Indonesian islands of Java and Sumatra, well-known for excellent coffee.

One of the civit's favorite foods is the red, ripe coffee cherry. They eat the cherries, bean and all, but they cannot digest the seed inside. That seed is what we call a coffee bean. While the bean is in the civit's stomach, it undergoes chemical changes and fermentations, enhancing the quality of the bean. The bean completes its journey through the civit's digestive system, and the still-intact beans are collected from the forest floor, cleaned, roasted, and ground just like any other coffee.

It's this relationship to the coffeefruit that made the "Civit Society" the name Bai uses for the company's best employees who are making significant contributions and inspiring others to do the same.

Every year, the company elects its top five people, and five flags featuring their faces hang from the ceiling. "It's all about the process of inspiring greatness in other people," says Weiss, named Entrepreneur of the Year in 2013 by the Princeton Chamber of Commerce. According to Weiss, the five qualities these five people possess: "They are audacious, authentic, tenacious, obsessive, and great."

Additionally, five is an important number at Bai. The company started with five people (employees now number more than 200), and the main brand is Bai5, with only five calories per serving.

(See the Resource section for the link to Bai's Super Bowl commercial, featuring Justin Timberlake and Christopher Walken.)

Material Handling Supply

In the B2B rather than B2C space is Material Handling Supply, Inc. (MHS Lift), a company that provides an extensive line of lift trucks, warehouse products, and material handling parts and services. Founded by two people in 1970 (now employing approximately 165), the company has consistently been recognized for its achievements in quality and service.

When brothers Andy and Brett Levin took over control of the company in 2013, they wanted to become more intentional about the corporate culture and further expand employees' desire to do business with the highest standards of ethics. I had the pleasure of visiting with President, Andy Levin to discuss the culture at MHS Lift and its impact on company performance.

Andy says that the process began by identifying the types of behaviors that they *didn't want*, and from there, they began to build out the positive attributes for the environment that they wanted.

As he puts it: "Culture is the personality of the organization. Customers do business with multiple touch points throughout our organization. It is critical that the experience, regardless of the type of interaction, be consistent, valuable, and pleasurable. It is also critical that employees feel free to try new things without the fear of failure. People should want to come to work each day and a healthy culture is the key to higher engagement."

Culture is "Fundamental"

Inspired by David J. Friedman's book, *Fundamentally Different* and its premise that an organization's culture is the primary driver of people's behavior, the cornerstone of the company's culture stems from a business card-sized, fold-out mini brochure entitled "The MHS Lift Way."

Inside the brochure is a list of 26 fundamentals that define the culture and the corresponding expected behaviors. For example, Fundamental #4 is "Walk in your Customers Shoes." The behavior associated with this is to "see the world from their perspective." The idea is to better understand their needs; however, that can be hard to do when looking at situations through your own lens.

Every employee carries the "The MHS Lift Way" Fundamentals on their person at all times, and every week, one employee is responsible for writing a short essay about what a particular fundamental means to them and how it has impacted their work.

If you're thinking that the employees must roll their eyes in frustration over the notion of having "homework," you're dead wrong. Andy's people take this very seriously and typically go above and beyond, by using quotes and other clever ways to depict the impact of the fundamental.

But that's not all.

This "Fundamental of the Week" is the starting point for every meeting that happens within the company that week in which the first 10 minutes are set aside to discuss the fundamental. Because these fundamentals are at the core of the company culture, all 26 are depicted in artistic fashion in every department location throughout the company, starting with main entry hallway as you walk into the building.

"MHS Lift has a spirit of collaboration where people can feel supported and know that their suggestions can impact real change. Our Fundamentals, The MHS Lift Way, clearly identify our guiding beliefs and act as a road map to solve challenges and make decisions. At MHS Lift, it is okay to have fun, make mistakes but not acceptable to make others feel self-conscious or bad about themselves." – Andy Levin, President

When customer service issues arise, employees are asked to take out their Fundamentals and consider which ones are applicable. Rather than ask management to provide solutions, employees are empowered to present their solutions. The Fundamentals are their guiding light for customer care as well as internal relations.

As Andy says, "You know that the culture is becoming part of the company's DNA when you overhear employees citing the Fundamentals and reminding one another that they work for a company that doesn't ascribe blame." From rooms that are designed to facilitate collaboration as well as comfort to the "no assholes" policy (which has been enforced!), the company takes their people and their culture seriously.

Instilling the culture into the employees' DNA doesn't take long. In fact, it starts on day one. New employees are welcomed to the company at a welcome party, complete with balloons. As Andy says, "It's not a party without balloons." The idea is that new hire paperwork is completed in the large dining area where employees come in to greet and welcome the new employee. When that employee goes home and is asked by family and friends, "How was our first day?" – the answer is, "They had a party for me!" Not a bad way to start.

Of course, the skeptics always ask about the impact to the bottom line. According to Andy, since he and Brett began implementing their corporate culture bedrock, within four years, revenue has doubled and profits have quadrupled; safety has increased and the company has received awards for being the #1 Crown Lift Truck dealer in two of the last three years.

Andy says: "Compared to our industry, our revenue and profitability per associate far exceeds the industry average. The culture changes implemented over the past few years has significantly reduced turnover which impacted profitability."

A Case of Corporate Cultures

Chapter Fifteen:

To B, or Not to B?

With Nella Bloom, Fraser Marlow, and Doug Claffey

To B, or not to B?

That is the question.

And many are answering with a resounding "Yes!"

I'm not talking about Shakespeare – I'm talking about B Corporations.

"It's Not Personal – It's Just Business."

If someone uses this term on you, to paraphrase the Urban Dictionary: You're about to be screwed. There are organizations that resort to this philosophy when making and conveying tough decisions. Often those decisions are based on simple economics. Occasionally those decisions specifically pertain to the economics of a reduction in staff.

Nella Bloom, Esq., Managing Member of the law firm Bloom & Bloom, LLC, is concerned about the destructive impact this philosophy has had on our communities. "Business is never just business," she says. "Behind every business decision is a person, or a set of people, who have their own motivations for the decisions they make. It's essential for owners to consider the impact – and the people impacted – by every business decision. These people are employees, customers, and the community at large."

For many consumers, "just business" no longer is good enough. Customers who want to encourage social impact can make their own decisions to patronize Benefit Corporations, otherwise known as B Corporations.

What Is a B Corporation?

A B Corporation is a for-profit company that must meet rigorous standards of social and environmental performance, accountability, and transparency. Most states, including Delaware, New York, California, Illinois, and Florida, have implemented rules to establish B Corporations. Some allow for other corporate forms as well, such as limited liability companies that adhere to similar rules.

B Corporations must adhere to a stricter standard than a typical corporation. Generally, a B Corporation's directors must consider the impact of decisions on employees, shareholders, customers, and the community at large. The B Corporation also typically must publish a report detailing its overall social and environmental impact as assessed against a third-party standard.

For example, Pennsylvania requires B Corporations to annually disclose (among other things) the public benefits they provide and the overall social and environmental impact made by the company during the year. B Corporations *pay* for the privilege of opening the kimono: There are fees to prepare the report, to file it with the Department of State, and to send it to their shareholders. Since each state makes its own laws, the standards for exactly what is required vary from state to state.

What is a Certified B Corp?

Once established under state law, the entity (whether it begins as a B Corporation or another type of entity) can apply for certification to become a "Certified B Corp." This certification, offered by the nonprofit B Lab (www.bcorporation.net), means that a corporation has met even stricter standards than required under state law. Additionally, a Certified B Corp must recertify every two years, so it has to continually strive to meet its goals of positive social impact.

B Corp is to business what Fair Trade certification is to coffee or USDA Organic certification is to milk.

The B Lab's vision is that companies will compete not only to be the best **in** the world, but the "*Best for the World*," and as a result, society will enjoy a more shared and durable prosperity.

B Corps meet the highest standards of verified social and environmental performance, public transparency, and legal accountability, and aspire to use the power of markets to solve social and environmental problems.

Today, there is a growing community of around 2,000 Certified B Corps from 42 countries and over 120 industries working together toward one unifying goal: to redefine success in business. (The link to the Certified B Corp Declaration of Interdependence is included in the Resource section.)

B Corp. Case Study

When Doug Claffey founded WorkplaceDynamics in 2006, he had ambitions to establish a rock-solid foundation of the new firm – one based on values and core principles.

At the time, many corporations were embracing the best practice of stating the core values that would guide the organization. But too often these statements were no more than pretty words on a glossy poster. The daily practices fell short of these lofty aspirations.

Fortunately, WorkplaceDynamics and B Lab started around the same time, and from the get-go, it was clear the two organizations were mission-aligned at deep level. WorkplaceDynamics signed on as a "Founding B Corp" the very first year certification was available and never turned back.

Over the last ten years, being a B Corp has been a significant part of "who WorkplaceDynamics is" according to Claffey. "We had clear values and purpose before formally becoming a B Corp, but ratifying our guiding principles has made them more concrete. Over time, as we have worked with multiple stakeholders, from clients to employees to investors, we have worn the B Corp badge with pride. We put it forward as a calling card, and it telegraphs our intent to put our mission first," says Doug.

How Much Does All This Social Impact Cost?

A Certified B Corp must work hard to meet its goals, and recertification can be costly – from $500 to $50,000 per year, based on revenue, according to the B Lab's website. Even if the corporation does not certify, a B

Corporation under state law still has to make regular reports to stakeholders, which run up costs in filing fees and legal fees. No matter what, it's likely *more* expensive to be a B Corporation than a typical corporation.

Then why be a B Corporation or a Certified B Corp? Why would a company pay more to be more heavily scrutinized? Why would it take on an affirmative obligation to do good for others?

Because it's not *"just business"* anymore.

Consumers don't just want goods and services. Consumers want environmentally conscious goods and community-oriented services. Many of us would prefer to patronize smaller companies even if the price were higher. We're willing to pay more for positive impact – for those companies to follow the Golden Rule.

Some companies want to become more attractive employers. B Corporations are attractive to millennials because of their open dedication to the greater good.

After all, a B Corporation must consider the impact of its decisions not only on its shareholders but also on its employees, the community at large, and the environment. So a B Corporation could be more likely to encourage its new fathers to take parental leave, or have a company-wide subscription to a bikeshare for its employees, or offer community service days. Not only do these features increase the number of qualified job applicants, but the successful applicants see the steps the B Corporation takes and believe in the company's mission.

According to Fraser Marlow, Head of Research at WorkplaceDynamics, "As with many human aspects of the enterprise, accounting for the value of being a B Corp is a challenge as so many of the benefits are intangible."

B Labs will point to the great business success of many registered B Corps indicating, if nothing else, that embracing a "triple bottom line" is by no means a hindrance to business success.

"Triple bottom line (or otherwise noted as TBL or 3BL) is an accounting framework with three parts: social, environmental (or ecological) and financial. Many organizations have adopted the TBL framework to evaluate their performance in a broader perspective to create greater business value."

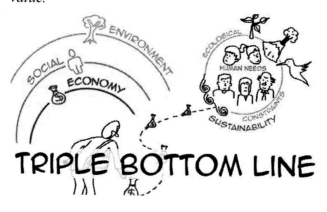

What WorkplaceDynamics discovered is that being a B Corp adds trust to every relationship: with employees, with investors, with clients and with the community at large. "It's hard to place a dollar value on trust, but at the same time we know that trust is invaluable," said Fraser. "Our board of directors, our customers, our employees all know that we stand for something more than just maximizing our profits. Even our suppliers acknowledge our B Corp status, with many of them extending the same discounts they would provide to not-for-profit organizations."

(A link to Workplace Dynamics' B Corp score card that is found on the B Labs website is included in the Resource section.)

Not Ready Yet?

Some companies can't take on these extra financial burdens, but still want to be socially conscious. And that's fine, too! Companies can do pro bono projects, or take on a day of service, or partner with a school, community center, or nonprofit to volunteer employee time.

Publicizing these efforts can have an immensely positive impact on sales without the financial burden of becoming a Certified B Corp – or even registering as a B Corporation under state law. They can also make the employer just as attractive an employer to possible applicants who want to believe in the social impact of their work. Even if your company is tiny, a shift in the principals' attitudes toward empathy, toward kindness – toward the Golden Rule – can make a huge difference.

To B, or Not to B

Chapter Sixteen :

Build Resilience to Build the Bottom Line

With Cheryl Hunter and Dave Nast

The ability to bounce back from adversity is an important quality to possess. This is true in sports, in business, and in everyday life.

Some people call this quality toughness; some call it grit. Another term for this quality is resilience.

re·sil·ience ◀)) [ri-zil-*yuh*ns, -zil-ee-*uh*ns]

noun
1. The power or ability to return to the original form, position, etc., after being bent, compressed, or stretched; elasticity.
2. Ability to recover readily from illness, depression, adversity, or the like; buoyancy.

There are vast bodies of research that delve into the linkages between being resilient, being happy, and having less stress. This also creates a positive feedback loop where being happy and having less stress increases your resilience. It's the type of Catch-22 that's worthwhile.

While resilience is not necessarily something with which you're hard-wired, it can be developed. On the personal level, that's good news. However, what does it mean to be resilient in business and what measurable benefit does that bring to the organization?

To understand what it means to be resilient and how that quality translates to the world of business, Workplace Behavior Expert and frequent contributor to The NEW ROI series and this book, Dave Nast, and I had the pleasure of visiting with renowned expert on resilience, Cheryl Hunter.

Cheryl Hunter is known as the go-to expert on resilience. She is a speaker, author, and high-performance coach who works with companies, schools, and individuals to help create transformative change. (Refer to the Resource section for a link to learn more about Cheryl.)

Cheryl learned resilience from her own experience. While traveling abroad as a teenager, she was abducted by two criminals who held her captive, assaulted her, and left her for dead. Hunter survived this life-changing event, turned her life around, and has dedicated herself to helping others to turn their lives and businesses around.

Cheryl is regularly called upon by major media to provide expert commentary, and her work has been profiled in CNN, *Fast Company*, *Forbes*, *U.S. News & World Report* to name a few. Cheryl's TED talks have been viewed hundreds of thousands of times. Her signature TED Talk is shared in the Resource section.

Becoming Friendly With Failure

Henry Ford said, "Failure is the opportunity to begin again more intelligently." Cheryl agrees, adding, "Resilient entrepreneurs and employees espouse the counterintuitive premise that the key to success is none other than failure."

Cheryl believes that there are "nuggets of gold" in every failure, and she encourages people to "hack your failures" by reverse engineering them to understand your common themes and responses so you can learn from your past failures.

Why Leaders Should Care About Resilience

Boxer, Mike Tyson once said, "Everyone has a plan until you get hit in the face." How you respond to that punch in the face takes resilience.

It's been said that there are only two certainties in this world: death and taxes. I would add another: **change**.

> *"Resilience is the ability to not only begin again after adversity but to do so with no loss of passion, purpose, or power"*
>
> *~ Cheryl Hunter*

The speed of business as well as the speed of life continues to accelerate rapidly, and that creates changes in how we work, how we communicate, how we travel, and how we receive information, just to name a few.

People need to be able to adapt and thrive amid constant change, so it doesn't come at them like the punch in the face that takes them out.

Smart leaders understand that elements of psychology and behavioral dynamics can have a tremendous impact on an organization.

For example, we've already demonstrated that organizations that foster a culture of trust earn higher returns and we've already demonstrated that happy people are more productive. Keeping people in these higher states of "best-self" really is good for business.

But Cheryl warns that while a positive mindset is helpful, happiness and positivity alone aren't the key to resilience, stating, "Blind-faith positive thinking doesn't serve anyone. That starts to verge upon magical thinking, which can actually make matters worse. As much as we don't like the fact, things can and will go wrong, and occasionally bad things happen to good people."

> *"The key of resilience is to move through failure with velocity."*
> ~ Cheryl Hunter

According to Cheryl, "If you can anticipate what will predictably go wrong, you'll be well-equipped to build a fail-safe plan to weather future failures."

Cheryl goes on to add, "This is critical thinking and planning that we can do either as individuals or collectively in an organization, business, or enterprise."

The Bottom Line on Resilience

Leaders who would contemplate an investment in resilience training and education would naturally want to understand the measurable ROI. According to Cheryl, the two biggest results are increased engagement and increased employee retention.

Employee turnover is not only disruptive, it's expensive. We've previously discussed the cost to replace employees, so it suffices to say that with increased retention comes the avoided costs associated with turnover. Avoided costs are bottom-line boosters.

Regarding engagement, we've previously discussed that Gallup finds that more than two-thirds of U.S. workers were not engaged in their jobs. As Gallup notes, "They are also more likely to miss work and change jobs when new opportunities arise."

Dave Nast provides the following sobering statistics regarding the impact of employee engagement:

- Disengaged workers cost the U.S. about $500B/year in lost productivity.
- 80 percent of employees who are dissatisfied with their direct manager are disengaged.
- 46 percent of new hires fail within 18 months; 89 percent of those failures are due to poor culture fit.
- Engaged employees are 31 percent more productive, create 37 percent more sales, and are three times as creative and innovative.
- Companies where the majority of the workforce is engaged improved operating income by 51 percent over companies with a majority of disengaged employees.
- Organizations with a higher number of actively engaged employees have an average of 147 percent higher earnings per share then the norm.
- Engaged employees are 87 percent less likely to leave a company than disengaged employees.
- Companies with a highly engaged workforce have 49 percent fewer accidents onsite.

As you can see, employee engagement has real economic consequences... so much so that I want you to reread and fully digest that list of Dave's statistics!

Learning resilience takes training, coaching, planning, and intention for people to be able to think logically and objectively at a time when our emotions are telling us to run for the hills.

Just like a seasoned fighter who has demonstrated resilience time and again can get hit in the face and execute their response plan for that potential outcome: We all need to learn how to pivot, counter-punch, get off the ropes, and get back to the center of the ring, so we can try again and re-focus our eyes on the big picture.

To clearly connect the dots: The biggest results of fostering resilience are increased engagement and increased employee retention. Keeping the sobering statistics about lack of both of those factors in mind, you can draw your own conclusion about the ROI of doing whatever it takes to increase the resilience of both your employees and ultimately your organization. I think you'll agree there is only one answer.

Be sure to watch Cheryl's signature TED Talk on resilience (link provided in the Resource section).

Chapter Seventeen:

The New ROI of M&A

With Laura Queen, Glen Hartenbaum, and Pam Prior

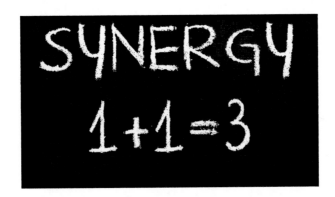

The math of M&A (mergers and acquisitions) looks something like the picture above, where 1+1=3.

The idea, of course, is that if Company A buys Company B, the sum of the combined parts will exceed the value of the individual components.

In valuation or corporate finance parlance, that's also referred to the realization of synergies.

But how often are these synergies actually realized and where do they come from?

The strategic objectives behind corporate acquisitions include the desire to enter new markets, acquire intellectual property, or gain access to key customer relationships, just to name a few. The synergies of combining two entities can range from things that enhance revenue to reducing expenses to entering new markets or consolidating operations. And more.

The hope is that once the acquired company is fully integrated into the operations of the buyer, those synergies will be realized and the deal will be accretive (i.e., positive from an economic perspective.)

Unfortunately, that doesn't always happen.

Even if you're not in the deal-making business, you may know that the failure of combined forces to synergize is true from your own experiences, and it derives from the basic principle that people are what make anything work. It's no different in realizing synergies.

You may have been with an employer that either bought another business or was acquired by another business. If you are nodding in agreement with the firsthand experience that "the deal didn't work out as planned," you're definitely not alone.

Depending upon the source of the data, there is evidence to suggest that between roughly 70 to 90 percent of M&A transactions fail to achieve their stated objectives. This includes failing to achieve the expected financial performance, meeting synergy targets, and meeting customer expectations. For example, a 2016 study published by Deloitte indicates that 84 percent of respondents' deals didn't generate the expected ROI.

Reasons cited as contributors to these failures

included insufficient due diligence processes, improper target identification, not valuing the target accurately, and failure to effectively integrate the combined entities.

While deal successes were indicated to be a function of the economic environment and, of course, proper valuation, effective integration remained the top-ranked factor by corporate respondents in achieving a successful M&A transaction.

What Does Effective Integration Look Like?

As we've said before, the value of a business is a function of how well the financial capital and intellectual capital are deployed by the human capital. So it makes sense that the key to effective integration begins and ends with the human capital: the people. The people both on the buying side and on the selling side.

To help me to better understand the impact of people in the M&A setting, I visited with Laura Queen, Managing Director of Colloquia Partners. With a doctorate in human and organizational learning, Laura and her team are experts at effective M&A integration. I also wanted to get the perspectives from the C-Suite, so I called on Chief Financial Officers and veterans of the M&A environment, Glen Hartenbaum and Pam Prior.

> *"By adopting an approach that places people front-and-center, you gain a number of important advantages."*
> *~ Laura Queen*

Laura explains that traditional approaches to M&A transition and post-merger integration adopt a strict project management framework for identifying, cataloging, and acting upon the tactical requirements of bringing two organizations together. There are significant merits to this approach, including the development of a comprehensive set of tasks necessary to ensure that the work of bringing two organizations together happens effectively and in a timely manner and that foreseeable risks are mitigated.

But Laura argues that there is a critical missing element in this approach: People!

Glen agrees and suggests that the acquirer has to take the time to consider the culture and interrelationships of the acquiree. Things to consider would include:

- What differences are there in the way the two companies work?
- How do they set priorities and solve problems?
- Do they have a lot of formal meetings or collaborate informally in small, ad-hoc groups?
- Are employees reserved and speak to each other professionally?
- Are they more informal and outwardly passionate?

These differences need to be acknowledged and considered.

Laura points out that by giving voice to crucial stakeholder groups, such as customers and most importantly, employees, you gain:

- **Insight into to your operation** – No one knows better how your organization operates than your employees. They are front-line in every aspect of your day-to-day activities.

- **Insight into your reputation and service levels** – Your customers know you better than you know yourself, and they are ultimately your bread-and-butter.

At a minimum, learning from and engaging these constituents in your discovery, diagnostics, change-management, and strategy-execution plans make all the difference in your eventual success or failure.

Furthermore, Pam adds that for this systems insight into the various stakeholder groups to be informative and drive the objectives, the acquirer needs to engage the individuals who make up that stakeholder group. They are more than just a part of the equation.

> *"The stakeholders aren't just a 'part of the equation,' they are the only ones who know how to make sense out of the equation."*
> ~ Pam Prior

Each one of them is not only affected (either positively or negatively) by the deal at hand, but each one of them has a career, a set of personal concerns, a life full of triumphs and defeats. And to access that person, you need to understand his or her context.

Both Pam and Glen explain that it is worth taking the time to look beyond just the employee number and seek to understand the *person* who is the employee. In the words of Teddy Roosevelt, "People don't care how much you know until they know how much you care."

As we've discussed previously, a happy employee is a more engaged employee; and a more engaged employee is a more productive employee. Genuine caring about employees builds trust, which fosters the buy-in to the corporate vision. As Pam says, "To succeed, you need people to give a damn."

A Case Study

The Colloquia team was recently involved with a buyer of a manufacturing business that recognized that employee retention would be key to a successful acquisition. Laura and her team divided the target company's employees into small focus groups of between three and ten people.

Participants in each focus group were asked to describe:

1) The strongest aspects of their work as an organization;
2) Where they had achieved their greatest successes;
3) What elements of their environment contributed most significantly to their long history of accomplishment; and
4) Who their most valuable team members were.

None of the interview participants identified themselves, individually, as critical to the success of the organization. They did, however, identify a team of mechanics and maintenance technicians as the most important employees to ensuring business continuity and successful manufacturing operations. Incidentally, such employees are very infrequently selected for retention bonuses.

Based on their findings, Colloquia developed and implemented a strategy for integration and employee retention. Here's what they've learned since:

At three months post-closing: The site had reduced its historic back-order levels from 40 percent to zero, had retained all but one employee (this one employee was a planned retirement), and had increased its production yield to 120 percent of target.

"In all of my acquisition experiences, human capital was the most critical success factor. And 'success' can look differently depending on how you assess the culture and the people being acquired."
~ Glen Hartenbaum

At seven months post-closing: The site was holding steady at 99 percent employee retention, had maintained its new zero (0) back-order levels, and was ending the year seven percent positive to their year-end financial targets.

At 12 months post close: The site was $2 million positive over their first 12-month financial projections and was outperforming their production capacity estimates by an average of 12 percent per month. An equally impressive outcome was the level of confidence this newly acquired team expressed in the ability of their new leaders to guide them to a positive future.

As Laura says, adopting a "people-centric approach" to transition during and following a merger or acquisition, or any major shift in an organization, affords the opportunity to build and reinforce aspects of an organization's culture in ways that promote employee engagement, and therefore, long-term value.

The "Real" Leaders

As we've observed in an earlier chapter, the real leaders or the rock stars of an organization aren't necessarily the ones with the titles or authority. These folks lead without being in charge.

Glen talks about situations he's seen in which the acquirer focused solely on the senior managers of the target organization. The staff that is the next level or two down was treated as nothing more than names on an organization chart. As he's experienced, some of those so-called "lower-level" people are likely to be the glue that holds the organization together.

While there is always pressure to achieve synergies and to achieve them quickly, Glen's advice for acquirers is to not rush the process of evaluating the individuals or you could lose good people.

Glen summarizes it succinctly when he says that "culture is hard."

He adds, "In all of my experiences, even if owners and managers of the acquired company stay on, and even if the acquiring company takes a hands-off approach, the culture of the acquired company will still change merely by having been acquired."

Pam adds that the "real" leadership in any organization is not necessarily represented by its organizational chart. With experience in Fortune 50 companies and pre-funding start-ups, Pam has learned firsthand that the people to be certain to identify are the real opinion leaders, or influencers, in the company.

Identifying these people in every organization she has worked with, Pam has built some of the most lasting friendships and organizational successes of her career. She attributes those successes to the teams who have engaged with her in the vision, and in most cases, that started with one influence-leader.

The Contribution Conundrum

Early in my career, my then-employer merged with another large institution. As a young and naive professional, I was surprised to learn that decisions about whom to retain in the newly combined company were being made by people who had never even spoken with the people who they were impacting.

Certain metrics that were unknown to most were apparently the key determinants. Managers were given the "cut list" by the higher-ups and instructed to make it happen. Fortunately, some of these managers saw the flaws in this system and had the courage to push back on this approach, saving many people's livelihoods and building tremendous rapport with their people that would span the years to come.

As a CFO, Glen has gone through several workforce valuation exercises in conjunction with acquisition accounting, so he understands how valuation professionals ascribe value to the workforce.

With a background in cost accounting, Glen has worked to allocate costs of indirect employees (e.g., customer service, procurement, accounting) to different products to try to determine the true profitability (versus gross profit) of everything his companies sold.

The problem, which Glen says he has yet to solve, is that all allocation methods reduce the work that people do to something that, while measurable, does not begin to capture the *value* that these people bring.

Sound familiar?

For example, Glen says that he can measure a customer service person by the number of sales orders that they process. But, he notes, that does not take into consideration much of the value that they add to the organization – like assisting the outside sales reps as they try to bring in new business; speaking with the customers to avoid or resolve problems; or anticipating customer needs and ensuring that the rest of the organization can meet those needs. The physical entry of an order, while easy to measure, is only a fraction of their day.

Bringing It All Together

It's been documented that most M&A transactions fail to live up to expectations, and it's also been documented that the primary reason for such failure is the lack of effective integration.

We've discussed what effective integration looks like and how it can be achieved. We've also discussed the positive economic impact of an effective integration.

> *"Every one of us, leaders, investors, customers, is being called upon to adopt a new approach to valuing people in organizations. There is growing movement to account for the tangible economic and human impacts resulting from and accruing to organizations on the basis of their approach to and treatment of people. The bottom line is: We can and should be doing well by doing good!"*
> ~ *Laura Queen*

Effective integration isn't about integrating systems or facilities. It's about integrating the people. They are the ones who will be handling those other integrations.

It's about understanding what drives people and recognizing them as human beings, not human capital assets. When people know that they are appreciated, they are more inclined to buy into the corporate vision and evangelize it to their colleagues.

Laura says that every one of us – leaders, investors, and customers – is being called upon to adopt a new approach to valuing people in organizations. There is growing movement to account for the tangible economic and human impacts resulting from and accruing to organizations on the basis of their approach to and treatment of people. The bottom line is: "We can and should be doing well by doing good!"

Chapter Eighteen:

Being Resilient in M&A

With Cheryl Hunter and Dave Nast

As we've just covered the importance of the human asset – people – through the process of an M&A and the importance of resiliency building, those two principles certainly intersect when a merger or acquisition occurs.

Whether through merger or acquisition, we've discussed the fact that most business combinations are considered to be failures from the standpoint of realizing the intended strategic imperatives of the deal. We've also discussed that the leading cause for these failures is the lack of effective integration.

When we talk about effective integration, we're talking about integrating the people in both organizations, as well as the respective corporate cultures. If you're one of the people who will remain in the newly combined company, you've got different decisions or considerations than someone who's been told that they are not in the plan after the transaction closes.

In either case, you need to be resilient in the face of these uncertainties.

Corporate Resilience – Surviving M&A

Companies being bought and sold are an everyday occurrence. While the goal of the transaction is the greater good for the organization as a whole, not everyone wins. Some may be forced to make tough decisions between what's best for their families and staying with the employer. Some may be impacted by having to start over and look for a new job. These are times when resilience is required.

Cheryl coaches her clients to be aware of the primitive, survival-instinct brain taking over in these circumstances.

When one's (financial) survival is at stake as the result of a merger, acquisition, takeover, downsizing, pay cut, or any other unwanted change, that is the time to  practice mindfulness and discerning the *actual* realities of the situation.

For instance: Is the stress-inducing circumstance in front of you real, or is it a function of your "survival brain" running away with you? Taking a moment to authentically assess the situation will help you move forward most effectively.

If the threat is a bona fide one, are you exacerbating the threat by adding unnecessary, unproductive worry, self-doubt, or other negative emotion into the mix?

A bona fide threat might look like you have been told that your position is being eliminated or the company is relocating and your spouse and children are unwilling to make the move. Conversely, the situation may simply be one which you don't prefer, and in the process, your "survival brain" takes over and tells you not to trust people or to get out while you can.

Cheryl says that it's in these moments that you need to be ruthless about discerning between what is actually happening in reality vs. our survival brain running away with us.

"A key component of resilience is the willingness to be accountable for one's own experience," Cheryl asserts. "If I am willing to re-frame whatever is happening inside an empowering context, I will stand a better chance of navigating the issue with a sense of grace and fortitude. Inside of this model, an individual chooses an empowering context not because one exists, but because devoid an empowering context, their experience suffers."

When Leaders Create Resilience

The principles of resilience that work with individuals are similar to those that work at the enterprise level.

Cheryl suggests that the C-Suite can empower their employees to be resilient by providing certainty, stability, safety, and the ability to contribute by doing work that matters.

"When those elements are present," Cheryl adds, "people create their own buy-in. They self-select as stakeholders and champion the company's cause as their own."

As with Maslow's Hierarchy of Needs, people need to get to safety before buying into the corporate "why." Corporately on Maslow's hierarchy, those attributes Cheryl listed (certainty and stability) fall on the "safety and security" level while the corporate "why" falls into the upper levels of self-esteem and self-actualization. The latter cannot be achieved without the former.

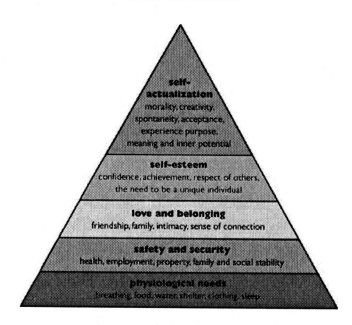

"When you empower your people to be resilient, they will get behind your mission. If your culture is one of scarcity and uncertainty, human nature dictates that your people will think of themselves first, even if that means undermining your mission." – Cheryl Hunter

In other words, when we are in survival mode, we are not always the best version of ourselves.

We can get caught up reacting, and when we are in that heightened emotional state, we are often challenged to discern what is actually happening before we can buy into a greater vision, mission, or plan until we feel safe.

Maslow's hierarchy is applicable to a company as it is to us as individuals. We cannot proceed to better and greater things until our base needs are met. Progress will only occur when individuals can rein in "survival brain" and accurately discern reality, and that can only happen when their base needs are met by the company.

Cheryl reminds us that when resilience is fostered in an organization, there is a greater buy-in and support for the corporate mission. There is no time when this is more critical than when companies are undergoing a transaction and will need to integrate two separate workforces and cultures.

Being resilient in the face of M&A means that the people-integration will go more smoothly, thus increasing the likelihood of a successful transaction.

Chapter Nineteen

The Return on Investment

With Frank DiBernardino

Whether for recruitment, retention, or because they really care, companies make significant investments in their people in excess of what's paid in salary and benefits.

From foosball tables in break rooms to formalized wellness programs, the dollars can add up fast.

But is there a measurable return on this investment (ROI)?

Good-to-Great-to-Gone

To get to the bottom of this, I spoke with Frank DiBernardino, the founder of Vienna Human Capital Advisors, an HR consultancy specializing in human capital analytics. Frank developed the *Vienna Human Capital Index™*, which isolated the total investment in human capital and quantified the ROI, productivity, and liquidity of the "people investment."

According to Frank, The Vienna Index was developed in response to a simple question asked by a CEO: "Are there credible ways to measure the financial performance of our investment in people?"

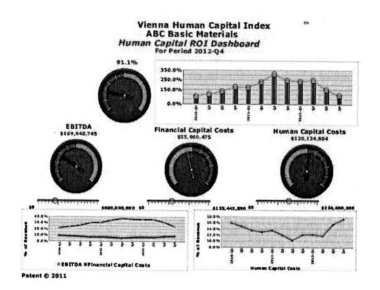

In Frank's book, *Optimize Human Capital Investments: Make the "Hard" Business Case*, he presents his patented formulas for determining the impact of human capital strategy on shareholder value.

As Frank notes, a business enterprise is comprised of financial capital and human capital, and: "While cash is the lifeblood of any business, it is **human capital**, the 'body' through which the lifeblood flows, that deploys the cash, and ultimately determines whether the deployed cash increases or destroys the value of the business enterprise."

While intangible assets like trademarks and patents are valuable business assets that help drive its value in the market, Frank notes that none of these assets would exist, however, without both financial capital and human capital. It is the **people** who developed the product or business method that was patented, or designed the process that drives the successful (or unsuccessful) product or service.

Said another way, human capital creates value for the organization by combining with other resources to generate capabilities.

Frank believes that two of the most vivid examples of the significance of human capital to the success and vitality of a business are Kodak and Circuit City.

In Jim Collins' book *Good to Great*, originally published in 2001, his team included Circuit City as a "Good to Great" company. At the time, it was clearly financially vibrant enough to meet the arduous criteria to be on this list. Eight years later, Circuit City was no longer in existence. Despite robust financial resources, the company folded after a series of disastrous management decisions.

Kodak, an iconic brand, at one time had a 90 percent market share of photographic film sales in the United States. Kodak began to struggle financially in the late 1990s as a result of the decline in sales of photographic film and its lack of speed in transitioning to digital  photography after having invented the core technology used in current digital cameras. The most recent year in which the company made a profit was 2007. In January 2012, Kodak filed for Chapter 11 bankruptcy protection. Again, the human capital failed to successfully guide Kodak through the disruptive photography market.

In both of these examples, the **people** in these companies squandered robust financial resources (cash and credit) ultimately resulting in liquidation in Circuit City's case, and Chapter 11 in the case of Kodak.

Human Capital "Expense"

What is the typical perception of the financial resources that companies spend on human capital – is it an expense or an investment?

Expenses are minimized and subject to cuts if business slows. Treating people as expenses, however, can prove costly. It wreaks havoc on performance and engagement. Productivity will take a hit when a business turns around and it becomes necessary to hire a group of new workers who will need time and training to get up to speed.

According to Frank, looking at the human capital spend as an *expense* drives an organization to think in terms of a cost-management perspective. Metrics such as total cost of the workforce as a percentage of revenue, or compensation and benefits as a percentage of revenue, foster a cost-management mindset. This is the natural tendency because of the way financial resources spent on human capital are treated from an accounting perspective – as expenses on the income statement.

And you won't find the money spent on human capital in the asset column of the balance sheet either.

This is in part due to accounting conventions, and in part due to the default view that is to think of the human capital spend as an expense.

Human Capital "Investment"

Conversely, if an organization views human capital costs as an investment, intended to drive revenue and profits, the perspective changes.

David Jardin, founder of the iTM System Group put it this way: "Assets are carefully chosen and held in the belief that they'll pay dividends and grow in value overtime. A company that views people as assets recognizes that costs to acquire, develop and retain talent are investments that pay off over time. So they're extremely cautious when downsizing."

If your perspective is that of an investor, you're inclined to ask the following types of questions:

- Is the human capital investment paying off in terms of ROI, effectiveness, productivity, and efficiency?
- How should we modify the human capital strategy to gain a greater payoff?
- Should we invest more or less, or redirect existing human capital investments?

"Talent should be managed carefully, invested in, and divested as appropriate; much the same as a portfolio of stocks." - David Jardin

While financial capital is vital to a business, human capital is the dynamic factor that ultimately determines the success of the enterprise. In short, the money spent on people (human capital) is an investment intended to drive both the revenue and profits of the business enterprise.

Chapter Twenty:

Putting It All Together

We've covered quite a lot of information to this point that is as complex and seemingly unquantifiable as human beings themselves. I feel it's worthwhile to take a moment to recap what we've uncovered.

Here's what we've discovered on this journey to understand the contribution of the human capital assets to the value of an enterprise:

- The valuation premise that the cost to replace people isn't a meaningful metric from the standpoints that (i) it doesn't tell the whole story, and (ii) it presumes that all people are the same.

- Rock star employees are everywhere in the organization. They are at all levels of the organization chart and they are not just the employees who are tied up with a Non-Competition Agreement.

- Rock star employees consider themselves to be difference makers, and they possess certain unique characteristics. Allow them to make a difference by playing to their strengths and their drives.

- Finding and retaining the rock star or purple squirrel employees is not a fantasy. You can predict who will be rock stars *before* you hire them. Additionally these people can be coached up to *super-productive* behavior.

- Aligning the organization's brand with its culture creates opportunities to thrive. It's like handing your people a metaphorical glass of Kool-Aid and having them drink it.
- Putting people in the proper role within their team increases productivity. Imagine having a Sorting Hat like the one from Harry Potter fame... role and fit are keys to high-performing teams.
- According to Gallup, 50 percent of employees left their job "to get away from their manager to improve their overall life at some point in their career."
- Innovation starts with trust. If people are fearful of criticism for thinking outside the box, they never will.
- We need to "hack our failures" to learn from them and demonstrate resilience to bounce back from them. Success is born from failure.
- Happiness fuels success, not the other way around. While people must choose this state, employers can create an environment that fosters happiness. Happy people are also 12 to 20 percent more productive... so it's worth the effort to create the environment.
- The vast majority of employees are disengaged; only about one-third of U.S. employees are engaged at work! The *real cost* of disengagement includes the collateral damage of disengaging otherwise good employees.
- When a disengaged employee becomes toxic, otherwise good employees are infected with the

disease. In fact, hiring a toxic employee is a worse economic decision than hiring a rock star employee by a factor of 2:1.

- Leadership's perspective will impact behaviors about how people are viewed and how they are treated. Shifting the perspective to view employees as *investments*, not expenses, will shift behaviors toward fostering an environment that improves engagement.
- Roughly 85 percent of M&A deals don't produce the desired results. The primary explanation for this statistic is because of poor integration of people and culture.
- Deal-savvy CFOs know from firsthand experience that for M&A transactions to succeed, management needs to embrace the view that people really are the most valuable assets and work hard to integrate both buyer and seller into a cohesive unit.
- An engaged workforce is more productive, and companies with more engaged workforces have proven to demonstrate greater profits and stock returns – *an almost three times better cumulative financial performance* than their industry peers!
- Forward-thinking leaders understand that the people really do drive the value of the organization.

Human Capital Financial Statements

The Human Capital Management Institute (HCMI) believes that there are ways to quantitatively measure human capital in the same way that generally accepted accounting principles (GAAP) provide a framework to quantitatively measure and report an organization's financial performance.

HCMI was founded on the belief that organizations can, and must, find better ways of measuring their investments in human capital. The workforce is the largest expenditure for most organizations, and while there are many time-tested ways to value the tangible inputs that drive all businesses, few exist to provide an accurate means to value and manage the workforce.

HCMI strives to set the North American and global standards in workforce analytics, workforce planning, workforce metrics and benchmarking, performance management, and HR data and transaction classification.

A white paper (the "white paper") by Jeff Higgins, Founder and CEO of HCMI, mentions, among other things, the issue that I raised early on in this journey. That being: That while there are disclosure requirements for companies to report on their various tangible and intellectual property assets, there are no such disclosures for their most valuable assets – the human capital. The workforce, often referred to as a company's most valuable asset, should not just be a period expense on the income statement but also an asset on the balance sheet. (Recall that in a purchase price allocation, the value of the assembled workforce is subsumed into goodwill.)

Dave Nast and I had the pleasure of visiting with Jeff to discuss the white paper and a variety of related topics.

The white paper makes the case that not only is the value of the human capital obfuscated, but perhaps more importantly, the risks associated with the human capital are obfuscated. The question posed:

"Would you invest in a company with 20 percent annual turnover in their management ranks? These companies turn over 100 percent of management every five years."

Knowing all of the costs associated with turnover, I suspect not.

HCMI has created human capital-based financial statements that are quite impactful. The Human Capital Asset Statement is predicated on the premise that the workforce creates value far greater than its cost.

HCMI adds: "It is generally accepted in business that human capital creates significant value beyond its cost. Otherwise, why would firms employ or contract with workers in a for-profit organization if they could not reasonably expect a significant return over and above their total cost? Even if we were to add one-time costs associated with hiring, paying, training, promoting or transferring the workforce, the workforce value still far exceeds its cost in a profitable business." This supports our early premise regarding the ***Cost-to-Recreate the workforce being an ineffective way to capture its true value***. There must be an element of ROI.

As Jeff added: "Most companies only realize the true value of their employees when those employees leave. Another problem with the Cost-to-Recreate is that people will accept below-market compensation to work in the right circumstances. When management needs to replace these employees, they will find that their actual costs are going to be much higher when they have to hire new employees at market rates (or higher). This impact gets magnified if the loss is of a high-performing employee who happens to be one of those who's paid at 70 percent of market.

The white paper also cites the work of Dr. Lauri Bassi, CEO, and Dan McMurrer, Chief Analyst, of McBassi and Company (in addition to other works) and demonstrates the relationship between investments in human capital and the value of a business by studying public company stock prices. What they found was that investments (not expenses!) in training resulted in "super normal" return on companies' investments in human capital.

Based on their research, they launched investment portfolios to prove that companies that invest significantly in training and developing their employees subsequently outperform the market. *__The portfolios outperformed the S&P 500 Index by an average of 4.7 percent per year.__*

Seeking a Change in Reporting Requirements

In July 2017, The Human Capital Management Coalition (HCM Coalition), a global group of 25 institutional investors representing over $2.8 trillion in assets, submitted a rulemaking petition to the U.S. Securities and Exchange Commission (SEC) urging the adoption of standards that would require listed companies to disclose information on human capital management policies, practices, and performance.

The following is excerpted in pertinent part from the press release announcing the petition:

> *The petition builds the investor case for enhanced disclosure while providing a foundation upon which the SEC can develop consistent and comprehensive standards that would allow investors to better understand and assess how well the companies they own are managing their talent.*
>
> *In creating a more robust reporting framework, the petition encourages the SEC to engage in a public standard-setting process that seeks input from all investors, the business community, and other stakeholders and interested parties.*
>
> *"As institutional investors and asset managers, members of the HCM Coalition have a vested interest in ensuring that the companies in which we invest are positioned for sustainability and growth over the long term," said Meredith Miller, Chief Corporate Governance Officer for the UAW Retiree Medical Benefits Trust. "The ability to effectively harness and apply the collective knowledge, skills, and experiences possessed by each individual in the workforce is essential to long-term value creation and is therefore material to investors evaluating a company's future performance. Current disclosures leave investors*

with an incomplete picture of how well companies are seizing opportunities and managing risks."

The petition does not define specific metrics for reporting; instead, the petition offers nine broad categories of information deemed fundamental to human capital analysis as a starting point to dialogue:

- *workforce demographics;*
- *workforce stability;*
- *workforce composition;*
- *workforce skills and capabilities;*
- *workforce culture and empowerment;*
- *workforce health and safety;*
- *workforce productivity;*
- *human rights; and*
- *workforce compensation and incentives.*

The HCM Coalition expects that specific data points will be developed as part of the rulemaking process, acknowledging that the relevance and applicability of some metrics may vary between industries and companies in the same industry.

"Workers are the bedrock of every successful company and the lifeblood of our economy. Talent is everything, and investors need to know how companies are managing their employees and whether they're quality, hospitable, and safe places to work," New York City Comptroller Scott M. Stringer said. "Human capital

management matters. Today we're taking the first step and starting that conversation."

The petition references a large body of empirical evidence that underscores the link between the effective management of human capital and better corporate performance across a number of metrics. Research has shown that investments in training and development, health and safety, employee engagement, diversity and inclusion and workforce composition, and staffing are associated with increased workforce productivity, reduced turnover, and higher customer satisfaction. Academic studies and literature reviews from Harvard, The Wharton School, and MIT, among others, also report evidence that better human capital management practices are associated with higher shareholder returns, profitability and overall firm performance against benchmarks.

Conversely, poor human capital management practices can create substantial risks for investors, including reputational and legal risks that can lead to depressed financial performance.

"Human capital management, done well, means investing in people in ways that allow them to develop and apply their talents to the organization," said Tim Goodman, Director, Hermes EOS. "A company that treats human capital as a vital asset, instead of a cost to be minimized, is not just a good corporate citizen – it is a good investment."

Investors believe the current SEC reporting system presents a critical information gap. Information that could help investors evaluate how well a company manages its workforce generally is not required in the U.S. markets and therefore can be hard to come by. Workforce-related disclosures mandated by the SEC are limited to employee headcount, preventing investors from gathering even basic information such as the amount of money a company spends on its workforce per year.

Everyone Can't Play 2ⁿᵈ Base

After working closely with my collaborating partners, I've gotten a greater appreciation for not only the importance of human capital but the role that leadership can have in either maximizing the return on that human capital or squandering those resources.

For the most part, people want to feel a sense of belonging – being a part of something bigger than themselves and want to make a difference. The roles and  responsibilities that they undertake, or are assigned to undertake, need to be in alignment with their interests and perspectives. It's not just the millennials who feel this way!

We can't underestimate the impact of perspective – a word that has appeared many times in this book. That's ultimately what differentiates the rock stars from the rest of the crowd, and quite possibly what put those people in the roles that *resulted in* them becoming rock stars in the first place.

> *"The only unique assets that a business has for gaining competitive advantage over its rivals are the skills and dedication of its employees."*
> ~ *Former Secretary of Labor, Robert Reich*

In the industry that I grew up in, it was believed, and often required, that each member of the team possess the identical skill sets and had to be excellent at each. *That's like starting nine second basemen on a baseball team.*

An effective baseball team needs a collection of players with varied skill sets – players who can hit for average, hit for power, some who can run fast, some who are excellent fielders. Those who can throw the ball accurately and with velocity might not be the best hitters, but you can't win without pitching, right? It's the blended talents of the team members that make the team successful.

As Jeff Higgins stated the concept: "Diamonds, like human capital, attain maximum value when flaws are minimized and facets are cut to optimally reflect light, working in concert with all other facets."

We don't all have to be great at the same things and it's imperative that leadership recognizes that. It's also imperative that leadership be in touch with their own perspectives and biases to understand how they can lead to poor decisions. A well-constructed team is a perfect example of the whole being more valuable than the sum of its individual parts. *And that performance is measurable.*

Like the smaller teams, the workforce is comprised of *individuals*, and every one of these individuals can impact the organization, either positively or negatively, so we need to also consider the softer issues like engagement, teaming, corporate culture, etc. into the mix.

We've discussed a variety of these intangibles throughout the preceding chapters, and we probably haven't even begun to scratch the surface. What has become clear, however, is that human capital management is rooted in psychology.

I'm a fan of Showtime's series, *Billions*, a drama about power politics in the world of New York's high finance. On the show, the fictitious hedge fund, Axe Capital, maintains an in-house psychiatrist / performance coach to help traders who find themselves stuck. This is a case of art imitating life, as in-house performance coaches are apparently not unheard of... and not just in the hedge fund world.

If you don't apply any judgment to the way Axe Capital is portrayed on the show, you can see that having the in-house resource for the individual employees can be a critical component to the organization's success. The stakes are high, and it's the people who drive outcomes that will either benefit or detract from the organization's success.

I'm not suggesting that companies hire psychologists and put them in every office. I'm trying to highlight that, as leaders, we sometimes need to act like psychologists. Remember too, that leaders aren't just people with prestigious titles; leaders aren't just in the C-Suite – leaders are everywhere in the organization.

Business relationships, like personal relationships, require similar interactions. We're all human beings and if you can think of your business relationships as, well… just *relationships*, you're off to a good start. You don't need a Ph.D.; sometimes you simply need to listen and be open.

As we've discussed, each person comes with their own perspectives, their own drives, and their own goals. Aligning each individual helps to align the entire organization.

"When people are treated as responsible human beings who have lives outside of their jobs and aren't nickeled and dimed about every hour they work, they tend to work their butts off for you. They value your respect and trust. They feel appreciated. And when these people feel appreciated, they tend to tell their nice, talented friends and acquaintances how great your company is, and sometimes those nice, talented people apply to work with you too." ~ Harry Gottlieb, founder of Chicago-based Jellyvision and Jackbox Games

You're in the Lifeboat, Too

Why should leaders care about any of this "hokum" when they pay their people to do a job?

For starters, historical data suggests that only one-third of the workforce is engaged. Let's put this into context.

Imagine that your organization is a lifeboat and there are ten people on board.

The three people in the front of the boat are engaged and rowing furiously to reach safety.

The four people in the middle of the boat have their oars in the water, but they are too distracted by the icebergs to coordinate their effort.

The three people in the back of the boat are trying to sink the boat.

Either you all survive or none does. You can see the value of engagement.

When I posed a similar question regarding the CEO's perception that "the employee's paycheck should be enough to keep them engaged," Jeff Higgins said, "I would ask a question back to that CEO: 'Is that really all it takes?' If so, then let's immediately cut one-third to one-half of all of the managers because what pay-only engagement strategy suggests is that training, career development, coaching, being part of a team, leadership, vision, the ability to make a difference, or support a higher purpose all have little meaning."

Additionally, Jeff notes that you manage what you measure and most organizations are absolutely atrocious at effectively measuring their human capital and the talent that lies therein. That would suggest that all too often they are also atrocious at managing their so-called most valuable asset.

Ouch. But true.

At a minimum, the no-brainer economics surrounding human capital investment can be summarized as follows:

- Anything that can be done to reduce turnover will avoid the costs associated with having to recruit and train new employees. This will also translate to profitability and increased valuation of the enterprise.

- Anything that can be done to improve employee engagement will translate to profitability and increased valuation of the enterprise.
- Increased engagement creates opportunities for people to do extraordinary things that will translate to profitability and increase valuation of the enterprise.

I want to spend a moment on that last point.

Al Cini gave me a splendid example of engagement as we were waiting to go on the air for my appearance on his show, *CEO Chat*. Al's premise is that if you manage people like inanimate objects, that is exactly how they will behave.

Picking up a paper cup, Al listed the "performance goals" for the cup being essentially:

- Prevent the beverage from leaking.
- Remain upright and stable.
- Maintain the temperature of the beverage for some limited period.

That's pretty much the expectations for the cup and we can clearly define its success.

Because you know what you'd like to see it accomplish, the cup would be considered to have failed its mission if it didn't do most of these things. The cup's upside performance, however, is limited. It doesn't have the ability to go above and beyond to exceed your expectations.

As Al said, "The cup isn't going to write a symphony or develop a process improvement to the supply chain."

Human beings, however, have the capability to do remarkable things and to *exceed expectations*. If they are managed like the cup, you'll likely get the minimum performance like that of the cup. But if you manage your people in a way that fosters engagement, they will have the unlimited upside potential to exceed expectations through discretionary effort.

The Most Critical Intersection

The value of a business is a function of how well the financial capital and intellectual capital are deployed by the human capital.

Right there, at the intersection of these three components, is where the magic happens.

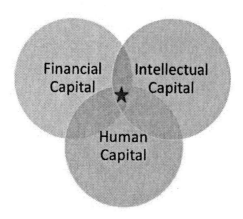

The good news is that there are tools and resources available for leadership that "gets it" or at least **wants to get it**. Engagement can be measured and programs can be implemented to increase it. Attitudes and perspectives can be changed for the positive and teams can be constructed that best utilize the collective talents of those individuals who comprise the team.

Employees know what impedes productivity or could improve the day-to-day processes in which they are involved. It would be wise to create the highest amount of trust possible to open the lines of communication, raise engagement and, with that, raise productivity.

So leaders, it begins with you. Listen to your people, because the people *ARE* the company. You've maximized the value of the workforce when each individual is happily engaged, demonstrating discretionary effort, acting as a champion for the company, believing in the bigger mission that is being served, and representing it like a walking advertisement. The return on those individuals is realized in a greater valuation of the business.

The value of a business is a function of how well the financial capital and intellectual capital are deployed by the human capital. So, you'd better get the human capital part right.

Putting It All Together

Chapter Twenty-one:

Putting a Number on It

When I started on this journey, my goal was to develop a way to actually put a numeric valuation on human capital and to determine what the actual "return on individuals" is.

Frank DiBernardino's work via the Vienna Index was revolutionary in thinking about the return on human capital investment because it redefined the denominator in the following equation:

Human Capital ROI = (EBITDA - Financial Capital Costs) / Human Capital Investments)

* EBITDA is earnings before interest, taxes, depreciation and amortization

A company's cost of capital reflects the company's cost of funding. The cost of capital will incorporate a company's cost of debt (raising funds through debt financing) as well as its cost of equity (cost of raising funds through equity offerings). Frank makes the compelling case that there must first be sufficient profit (EBITDA) to cover a company's cost of capital. Each dollar of profit above the cost of capital is therefore attributed to the human capital investment.

From this premise, Frank isolated the human capital investment to include three key components:

- Employee costs
- Costs in support of employees
- Costs in lieu of employees

In valuing the assembled workforce, we have modified the more traditional Cost-to-Recreate model to include these indirect costs that Frank suggests. Recall that the Cost-to-Recreate only really considers direct costs, so adding the costs to support employees and the costs in lieu of employees provides a better big picture. This gets us more meaningful insights on the workforce in the aggregate, but we need to also consider the impact of the difference makers in the organization. Taking this Cost-to-Recreate a step further, the use of employee-engagement surveys on a regular basis will help to identify and clarify exactly who the **rock star** employees are. (The solutions mentioned throughout this book are also great tools to identify, manage, and maximize the human capital investment.)

In assessing an individual's performance, their contributions of discretionary effort – the going above and beyond – is also an indicator of engagement. For these engaged employees, a premium would be warranted above their total cost to capture their positive contributions, but as Jeff Higgins of HCMI reminds us, that premium would need to be capped based upon the nature of the position. For example, a core, high value-added role (e.g., interacts with customers, impacts pricing, operational or strategic decision making) would command a larger premium than a non-core, low value-add role (e.g., largely administrative yet important to operations).

For the disengaged employees, logic would suggest that a discount would be warranted. It would also be important to identify those who have moved across the spectrum to actually becoming toxic. Using a medical metaphor, these employees should be quarantined to determine their ability to be rehabilitated. If they cannot be rehabilitated, their cost to the organization over time would be too great to justify retaining them.

For those employees who are in that middle-ground, they are clearly less productive than the rock stars and consequently contribute less value to the organization. But, as we've discussed, with the right leadership they can become more engaged and thus more productive.

The Impact on Business Enterprise Value

Even though companies are not currently required to record the value of their human capital assets on the balance sheet, the preceding should not be dismissed as simply an academic exercise. Understanding the *true* value of the assembled workforce and the contributions of *true* key individuals will allow management to better allocate financial capital to the human capital assets. As we've been reiterating throughout the book and, indeed, as the initial premise: human capital is the most critical asset  in every organization and effective management is worth every dime. We're striving to move this beyond an inherent, gut feeling.

Beyond the granularity of putting a "real number on people" is the overarching concern about understanding the impact of the human capital assets on the overall valuation of the business enterprise. That's where, for many, the rubber meets the road.

I want to re-emphasize Frank DiBernardino's observation that there must first be sufficient profit to cover a company's cost of capital, where each dollar of profit above the cost of capital is therefore attributed to the human capital investment. It's also worth reiterating that HCMI offered a similar assessment. To better understand the implications of the cost of capital, we'll need to take a brief dive into some valuation concepts.

The premise of business valuation is that it is *forward looking*, where value of a business (today) is equal to the present value of its expected future benefits, like cash flow. These estimated future benefits are converted into a current value through a mathematical technique known as discounting. The discount rate that is applied to the future benefit stream typically is the company's cost of capital, as defined previously. Considering the relative proportion of debt-to-equity in a company's capital structure is called the weighted average cost of capital ("WACC").

WACC is defined by Investopedia as *a calculation of a firm's cost of capital in which each category of capital is proportionately weighted. All sources of capital, including common stock, preferred stock, bonds and any other long-term debt, are included in a WACC calculation.*

$$WACC = (Ke * \%e) + (Kd * \%d)$$

Where:

Ke = cost of equity, Kd = after tax cost of debt,

%e and %d = proportion of equity/debt based on market value

Hang in there with me, I'm not going to turn this into a finance class, but by unpacking the above formula just a bit, the cost of equity component (Ke), using the Capital Asset Pricing Model is as follows:

$$Ke = Rf + (\beta \times RPm) + RPs + CRP + CSRP$$

Where:

Rf = risk-free rate, β = beta, RPm = market risk premium, RPs = size premium, CRP = country risk premium, CSRP= company-specific risk premium

That's it for symbols and equations. Here's what's important:

Investors want to be compensated for risk: The more risk associated with the investment, the higher the expected / required rate of return ("cost of capital" or "discount rate").

The higher the discount rate that gets applied to the future benefit stream, the lower the value of those future benefits.

Each of the individual components in the cost of equity calculation is market-based and supported by empirical data. All but one... and that is: the company-specific risk premium (CSRP).

There is debate in the valuation community as to whether adding this company-specific risk premium is double counting factors considered in the other components, but it is still widely accepted that there are risks inherent to a specific business that are not captured elsewhere in the cost of equity inputs. Thus, this adjustment is warranted.

Some of the factors that valuation professionals consider when developing the CSRP include:

- Revenue and profitability growth trends
- Company financial risk
- Operational risks
- Customer, product and market concentration
- Relative competitive position
- Quality and depth of management team

Unlike the other variables, there are no market-based or empirical studies to refer to when estimating the adjustment factors for these elements. So, the assessment of these, and other factors, results in a ***subjective adjustment*** to the discount rate based on the professional's experience and judgment.

As noted in the HCM Coalition petition: *"Greater transparency would allow investors to more efficiently direct capital to its highest value use, **thus lowering the cost of capital for well managed companies.**"*

All other things being equal, a lower cost of capital (discount rate) will increase the valuation. A higher discount rate lowers the valuation. The greater the impact of the CSRP, the bigger the impact on cost of capital and on the valuation.

Thinking about the McBassi portfolios and the diverse topics that we've discussed in this book, I believe that the human capital investment, or lack thereof, must be considered in the determination of the CSRP, effectively adding another bullet point to the list above.

Many valuation professionals only give consideration to the depth and quality of the subject company's management team when thinking about the human capital component in developing a CSRP; however, *all* human capital assets should be considered.

Note that this could prove to be risk-mitigatory, thus lowering the company's cost of capital and ***increasing*** its valuation.

There is more work to be done on this, but perhaps there is an iterative process that can be applied, whereby we can consider the human capital investment factor ("HCIF") component in the calculus.

So, the equation, modified to consider "The NEW ROI," might look something like this:

$$Ke = Rf + (\beta \times RPm) + RPs + CRP + CSRP\ (-/+HCIF)$$

in which HCIF becomes part of CSRP

The HCM Coalition's petition to the SEC makes a compelling case for the types of disclosures that would allow for relative comparisons to the guideline public companies that valuation professionals would use as benchmarks to quantify and document any such adjustment to their privately held subject-company clients.

I discussed this concept with Jeff Higgins of HCMI, and he indicated that "the concept of the HCIF makes a great deal of sense. We are at the early stages of having the ability to collect the necessary data to develop the idea further. If the SEC mandates public company disclosures around human capital investment, we might just be able to calculate the impact on a company's cost of capital."

It would also be interesting to observe the performance of the public companies' stock price performance over time on a pre- and post-disclosure basis to quantify the market's response to these disclosures and the resulting impact on valuations.

Given that it is documented that the companies that are perceived to be dedicated to investing in human capital outperform their peers, my suspicion is that with increased transparency and data related to this topic, we'll see a direct correlation between human capital investment and stock price performance (i.e., the business valuation.)

An accounting update contained in the August 2017 edition of *Business Valuation Update* published by Business Valuation Resources discusses the notion of it becoming a new world under the Financial Accounting Standard Board's (FASB) "Definition of Business" rules that are scheduled to be implemented in 2018. It is expected that under these new rules, which clarify the definition of what constitutes a business, there will be more asset acquisitions and fewer business combinations in the future. Because of this shift in emphasis to asset acquisitions, the article states that there will be two new areas of scrutiny.

The first area of scrutiny is the company's workforce value, which must be recognized in an asset acquisition. Adam Smith of PriceWaterhouseCoopers, and formerly with the FASB, was quoted in the article as saying, "We probably don't do a great job at valuing the workforce, so we may want to think about this."

The second area of scrutiny is the non-competition agreement. Some consider the Non-Compete to be a separate transaction while others consider it to be a part of a business combination. Perhaps in re-visiting the significance of the non-competition agreement, a case can be made for valuing those rock stars who are *not* encumbered by such an agreement.

There is a growing momentum toward a convergence of new SEC reporting requirements regarding human capital matters along with a corresponding shift in the accounting / valuation implications for human capital. If this convergence materializes, we might just be really headed into a whole new world!

Just Getting Started

We all have our intuitions regarding the relationship of the human capital to the impact on business valuation, and there are empirically documented bodies of research that support what we've always known to be true. Mandated disclosures like those sought by the petition would pave the way for irrefutable, quantifiable evidence of *The NEW ROI: Return on Individuals.*

Regardless of the success or failure of the petition and whether or not the equation is changed (and whether or not you paid any mind to the actual equations), the real conclusion is that human capital – quantified or not – is the ultimate driver of every successful and profitable organization. How management approaches, embraces, encourages, and appreciates the human capital asset is truly the lynchpin to each and every organization!

Please keep your comments and emails coming, and I would respectfully ask anyone who has the inclination and resources to explore this subject share their findings. We're just getting started.

We'll be working hard to identify and present case studies, so stay tuned. In fact, if you or someone you know has gotten serious about corporate culture and the value of people and would like to be considered as a case study, please have them contact me through LinkedIn.

To learn more about The NEW ROI: Return on Individuals, or to get involved, please join our on-line communities on LinkedIn:
https://www.linkedin.com/groups/7024279
and on Facebook:
https://www.facebook.com/TheNEWROIReturnOnIndividuals/

Also, check out the two bonus chapters at the end of the book!

Acknowledgments

I want to thank all of my collaborating partners and the friends of this project for their contributions and inspiration. It has been such a pleasure and an honor to team with you.

A big thank you to EisnerAmper CEO, Charly Weinstein for writing the foreword of this book.

Thank you's also go out...

To A – for your unwavering support and inspiration – anything can happen.

To the "other Dave" – a rock star, even without the mullet.

To Obi-Wan – it's nice to have a Jedi Master on my side.

To my children, Rex and JR – who had to learn about resilience early and often.

To Rena, Bookie and the T's – for modeling great leadership for all.

Special thanks to my editor, Ann, for making this project a reality.

I would also like to thank all the people who are making a difference in their organizations and to those leaders who recognize that "people really are an organization's most valuable asset."

This book is dedicated to the memory of David Jardin, founder of the iTM System Group, who inspired me to start this journey.

Contributors

Chris Mercer, Valuation Expert and CEO of Mercer Capital

Z. Christopher Mercer is the founder and Chief Executive Officer of Mercer Capital. He has prepared, overseen, or contributed to hundreds of valuations for purposes related to tax, ESOPs, buy-sell agreements, and litigation, among others. Chris is a prolific author on valuation-related topics and a frequent speaker on business valuation issues for national professional associations and other business and professional groups. His latest book, _Unlocking Private Company Wealth: Proven Strategies and Tools for Managing Wealth in Your Private Business_ was published by Peabody Publishing. Follow Chris on Twitter @ZChrisMercer.

Jeff Higgins, Founder and CEO of Human Capital Management Institute

Jeff Higgins is the Founder and CEO of the Human Capital Management Institute. Jeff is a global thought leader with 25 years' combined workforce planning, analytics and finance experience supporting Fortune™ 500 companies. He has helped organizations around the world quantify the ROI of workforce decisions and realize cost-saving opportunities of up to $1.0 billion USD. Jeff is both a former senior HR executive and former CFO, and a regular speaker at HR events. Previously, Jeff worked in finance at

Johnson & Johnson, Colgate Palmolive, Klune Industries and a senior HR leader at Countrywide Financial, IndyMac Bank, and Inform, a leading analytics software company. Jeff is on the SHRM Global Standards Committee on human capital, the Center for Talent Reporting board and founding member, PwC Saratoga Institute advisory council. Connect with Jeff on LinkedIn and follow him on Twitter @metricsman1.

Marla Tabaka, Business Coach and *Inc.* Magazine Contributor
Marla Tabaka is a small-business adviser who helps entrepreneurs around the globe grow their businesses well into the millions. She has more than 25 years of experience in corporate and startup ventures and speaks widely on combining strategic and creative thinking for optimum success and happiness. Marla is also a writer for *Inc.* Magazine, as well as co-host of *The Big Pitch Radio Show* with Kevin Harrington (one of the original sharks on ABC's *Shark Tank* and founder of *As Seen on TV*). You can follow Marla on Twitter @MarlaTabaka.

Dave Nast, Managing Partner of Nast Partners
David B. Nast owns Nast Partners and is a Workplace Behavior Expert and an award-winning Certified Business Coach with over 25 years of experience in Executive Coaching, Leadership

Development, Talent Management, Training, Career Coaching, Executive Search, and Human Resources Capital Management. He has coached thousands of CEOs, business owners, and executives. For additional insights from David, visit his LinkedIn Pulse Author Page and follow him on Twitter @DavidBNast. You can also subscribe to David's blog at Huffington Post.

Candida Seasock, Founder of CTS & Associates
Founder and President of CTS Associates, LLC, Candida Seasock is an innovative business adviser, specializing in enabling client growth and management success through internal executive teams and/or advisory boards that support vision, innovation, change that supports operation, finance, and technology and employee growth. Ms. Seasock is best known for her work in building high-value market recognition for mid-size companies. She rejects the transactional mentality in business and refrains from working with companies that do not value and respect the inherent human aspect with employees and customers. To confirm Ms. Seasock's approach, many of her best clients have achieved Fastest-Growing company awards. Candida can be contacted at pjscts@comcast.net.

Dr. Michael Housman, Co-Founder and Chief Scientific Officer for RapportBoost.AI

Michael Housman is the Workforce Scientist in Residence at HiQ Labs where he mines publicly available data for insights that allows large employers identify employees who are potential flight risks and take actions that will help retain them. He has published his work in a variety of peer-reviewed journals, presented his work at dozens of academic and practitioner-oriented conferences, and has had his research profiled by such media outlets as *The New York Times*, *Wall Street Journal*, *The Economist*, and *The Atlantic*. You can follow Michael on Twitter @MichaelHousman and on LinkedIn.

Beverly Borton, Founder of Bev Borton Coaching

Beverly Borton, Founder of Bev Borton Coaching, is passionate about helping people reveal their hidden potential. She partners with clients in a thought-provoking and creative process that moves them to maximize their personal and professional possibilities. She creates experiences for groups that enable participants to explore what matters most, then focus on actions that serve their highest aims. Her clients include business owners, management teams, entrepreneurs, performing artists, and consultants.

Art Dimitri, Founder of Innovation25

Art Dimitri, is the founder of Innovation25 — a management consultancy that helps growing companies grow faster by focusing all their activity solely on their customers. He has previously held leadership positions at a number of technology companies including CA Technology, PLATINUM technology, Aston Brooke Software and Zenith Data Systems. He has served the community as a Board member of the American Society of Inventors and Vice-Chairman of the Greater Philadelphia Senior Executive Group Innovation Leadership Forum.

Monique Caissie, Speaker, Facilitator, Consultant, Coach

The most successful leaders are not infallible when faced with someone who "drives them crazy!" Monique Caissie's strategies to go from conflict to collaborations are appreciated by all who meet her. As a speaker, facilitator and consultant and coach, Monique draws from 30 years of crisis intervention work to help others improve their results while feeling more heard, respected and happier. She is an Accredited Trainer for DISC as a Human Behavior Consultant and a Certified NLP Professional Coach. Check out her website, join her professional network on LinkedIn or check out some of her articles on *Huffington Post*.

 **Stephan Seyfert, Business Advisor and Founder of Pentimenti LLC**
Stephan Seyfert helps move people to take beneficial action. Sometimes that's called "leadership development," "success coaching," or "truth speaking." Other times it's called "sales," "communication," and "marketing." By any name, it's about understanding the psychology of action and what motivates people to do what it takes to achieve the success they desire – no matter what fears or obstacles stand in the way.

As an entertaining and engaging presenter, Stephan also teaches others how to master these skills. This is often called "training," "teaching," or "speaking." Having never known stage fright, Stephan just calls this "value-adding fun."

Usually involved in multiple projects and partnerships with leaders around the world, Stephan has become an internationally sought-after resource; a sort of "secret weapon" for creating and maintaining greater success (and, sometimes, rebuilding it). He's been a journalist, editor, author, marketer, consultant, mentor, speaker, nonprofit board member, and entrepreneur. He was even a U.S. Navy Seabee. He's been called a non-conformist, a rule-breaker, and a quipster. Despite having a satirical bent and sometimes dark humor, he's even been called open, authentic, and caring. What Stephan enjoys most, though, is when his daughter calls him "dad." You can follow Stephan on LinkedIn.

Dr. Janice Presser, CEO of The Gabriel Institute and Teamability.com

Dr. Janice Presser is CEO of The Gabriel Institute and Teamability.com. As a behavioral scientist and architect of the technology that powers Teamability®, she has studied team interaction in academic, clinical, and business settings for over 25 years, and has shared her expertise in the areas of HR metrics and measurements, workforce planning, and human capital assessment. Including the 2017 release of *Timing Isn't Everything, Teaming Is.*, Dr. Presser has authored seven books and myriad articles on various aspects of teaming, from parent/child, to personal and family relationships, to workplaces and spiritual communities.

In an era of digital disruption and transformational change, Dr. Presser's integrated technology and management methods are being used to design collaborative cultures, to produce extraordinary business results, and to open new pathways to meaningful work and organizational health. You can follow her on Twitter @DrJanice, connect with her on LinkedIn and Facebook, read her answers and opinions on Quora, and view her TEDx talk.

Al Cini, President of Al Cini and Partners

Al Cini founded Al Cini and Partners to help companies solve the productivity dilemma. Al believes that, at the heart of every successful organization, there exists a signature positive role model (he calls this a

Role Target) that expresses, in the ideal, its shared Brand (Behavior) and Culture (feelings: i.e., attitudes and beliefs). Leveraging decades of research into the behavioral determinants of organizational performance, his Brand and Culture Alignment Toolkit includes instruments that help organizations discover their Role Target and methods that use it to enhance engagement, boost productivity, and improve performance. You can follow Al on Twitter @AlCini.

Andy Levin, President, MHS Lift, Inc.

Andy Levin is the President of MHS Lift, Inc., a leading provider of materials handling products and services in the Greater Philadelphia area. After spending over two decades working in every department of the company, Andy and his brother Brett purchased the business from their father in 2012. Embracing a commitment to excellence, innovation, a dignified work environment and ethics, Andy has championed an increased role of positive organizational values to build a culture of success. MHS Lift, Inc. is the recipient of the 2014 and 2016 Crown Summit Award and the 2016 Crown Pioneer Award given to the number one dealer in the country. Andy holds a degree in Economics and Political Science from the University of Delaware. He is a member of the Philadelphia Chapter of YPO and an Executive Board Member of the Katz JCC. Andy lives in Cherry Hill with his wife and three daughters.

Nella Bloom, Managing Member, Bloom & Bloom

Nella Bloom is the Managing Member at the law firm of Bloom & Bloom. Nella specializes in helping small and emerging businesses organize and reach their potential. From starting up a business, purchasing and protecting assets, and starting off on the right foot, to thinking about next steps, Nella helps clients think through their options. Follow Nella on Twitter @NellaMBloom.

Fraser Marlow, Head of WorkplaceDynamics Research

Fraser Marlow heads up WorkplaceDynamics research and marketing efforts. As the author of many articles on the topic of employee engagement and coaching, Fraser brings a broad perspective on how organizational culture impacts business results. Fraser is co-author of *The Engagement Equation* (Wiley 2012), a comprehensive senior executive guide to building stronger engagement strategies and is a frequent speaker at conferences and events, sharing the many insights from ten years of studying Top Workplaces. Follow Fraser on Twitter @frasermarlow

Doug Claffey, CEO and Co-founder of WorkplaceDynamics

Doug Claffey is the chief executive officer and co-founder of WorkplaceDynamics, a leading provider of technology-based employee engagement solutions that help organizations unlock potential, inspire performance, and achieve amazing results. He led Best Companies in the United Kingdom and held leadership positions at General Electric, Analytical Graphics, and McKinsey & Co. Doug is a highly regarded presenter, including dozens of Top Workplaces events across the United States, the Microsoft Convergence Conference, and as a featured guest on shows such as "Leadership in Action" for SiriusXM Business Radio. Doug received his master's degree from the University of Pennsylvania and a bachelor's degree from the University of Delaware. Follow Doug on Twitter @dougclaffey.

Cheryl Hunter, Best-Selling Author, Speaker, Resilience Expert
The go-to expert on resilience, two-time bestselling author Cheryl Hunter was just a teenager when she was abducted by two criminals who eventually left her for dead. Cheryl survived this life-changing trauma, refocused her life, and found freedom.

In the process, she created an educational framework that empowers anyone to overcome adversity. Her framework has been profiled by *PBS*, *Forbes*, *Huffington Post*, is highlighted in her four TED talks, and is taught worldwide by Cheryl and her team at The Hunter Group. Cheryl has helped over a quarter million people turn their lives around and create lasting change.

She also provides expert commentary regularly across major broadcast and cable networks including *CNN* and *HLN*. To contact Cheryl or to learn more, visit www.CherylHunter.com. You can also follow Cheryl on Twitter @HunterCheryl and like her on Facebook.

Laura Queen, Founder and Managing Partner, Colloquia Partners

Laura Queen is the Founder and Managing Partner of Colloquia Partners. For more than 20 years, she has been entrusted with activating M&A through senior executive roles within firms across the pharmaceutical, retail, banking, technology, and agricultural industries. She's also worked in the public sector.

Laura's focus on the people-side of M&A transaction services includes due diligence, post-merger integration, cultural alignment/organizational restructuring, and performance consulting to enhance leadership, team, and organizational outcomes. Laura and her team view people as a company's biggest source of value and specialize in helping organizations realize substantial wins with this focus in mind. Connect with Laura on LinkedIn, follow Laura and her team on Twitter (@colloquiaprtnrs) and like them on Facebook and LinkedIn.

Glen Hartenbaum, Chief Financial Officer

Glen Hartenbaum is a Chief Financial Officer with more than 20 years of finance and accounting executive experience with middle market, privately held companies. He also has experience managing human resources and information technology.

Glen has worked in a variety of industries including manufacturing, distribution and professional services. He is also a Certified Public Accountant. Connect with Glen on LinkedIn.

Pam Prior, Founder and CEO, Priorities Group Inc.

Pam Prior is the founder and Chief Executive Officer of Priorities Group Inc. A CPA and CFO, Pam has worked with start-ups to Fortune 50 companies. She has participated in and led organizational transformations across multiple industries during periods of major change, including crisis-level situations, rapid growth, and under significant resource constraints.

Pam is currently disrupting the market with a new CFO Services model for entrepreneurs, enabling small business owners to access (affordably) elite financial leadership. Known as The CFO Quarterback to Allstar Entrepreneurs, Pam is host of the WCKG-Chicago's weekly radio show (and podcast), *Cash Flow*, and author of the #1 international best seller *Your First CFO: The Accounting Cure for Small Business Owners.*

Frank DiBernardino, Founder, Vienna Human Capital Advisors

Frank DiBernardino is the Founder of Vienna Human Capital Advisors; an author and developer of the patented Vienna Human Capital Index.™ Frank, for the first time, isolated the total investment in human capital and quantified the ROI, Productivity and Liquidity of the "people investment."

Frank writes a blog on human capital analytics for *The Conference Board* and he has also had articles published in *Directors & Boards* magazine, *Directors & Boards* E-Briefing and *People & Strategy* (HRPS peer review journal) on measuring the economic value of companies' investment in human capital.

Connect with Frank on LinkedIn, and be sure to check out Frank's book, *Optimize Human Capital Investments: Make the "Hard" Business Case.*

Contributors

Resources

Chapter 1: The Value of the Workforce
High Cost of Turnover:
Center for American Progress:
www.americanprogress.org/issues/labor/report/2012/11/16/
44464/there-are-significant-business-costs-to-replacing-
employees/

Chapter 2: The Difference Makers
John Maxwell, *The Difference Maker*
http://store.johnmaxwell.com/The-Difference-
Maker_p_692.html

OC Tanner Institute:
www.octanner.com

David Sturt, *Great Work: How to Make a Difference
People Love*
www.amazon.com/Great-Work-Make-Difference-
People/dp/0071818359

Chapter 3: Want to Be Successful?
Angela Duckworth, *Grit, The Power of Passion and
Perseverance*
http://angeladuckworth.com/

TED Talk: Angela Lee Duckworth: "Grit: The Power of
Passion and Perseverance."
www.ted.com/talks/angela_lee_duckworth_grit_the_power
_of_passion_and_perseverance#t-260417

Determine your Grit Scale:
http://angeladuckworth.com/grit-scale/

Chapter 5: In Search of the Purple Squirrel

The Predictive Index:
www.predictiveindex.com/the-predictive-index

References:

Harris T., Tracy, A. & Fisher G. (2011). *Predictive Index® Technical Overview*. © 2011, Praendex, Incorporated, d.b.a. PI Worldwide. All rights reserved.

Hunter, J.E. (1983). "A casual analysis of cognitive ability, job knowledge, job performance, and supervisor, ratings." In E Landy, S. Zedeck, & J. Cleveland (eds.), *Performance Measurement and Theory* (pp. 257-266), Hilldale, N.J.: Erlbaum.

Hunter, J. & Hunter, R. (1984). "Validity and utility alternative predictors or job performance." *Psychological Bulletin*, 96 (pp. 72-98).

Smith, F. & Hunter, J. (1998). "The validity and utility of selection methods in personnel psychology: Practical and theoretical implications of 85 years of research findings." *Psychological Bulletin* 124, (pp. 262-274).

Smith, M. & Smith, P. (2005). *Testing people at work- Competencies in psychometric testing.* Blackwell Publishing UK. All rights reserved.

Chapter 7: Happiness or Success: Which Comes First?

TED Talk: Shawn Achor: "The Happy Secret to Better Work."
https://www.ted.com/talks/shawn_achor_the_happy_secret_to_better_work?language=en

Gallup: Worldwide Employee Engagement
http://www.gallup.com/businessjournal/188033/worldwide-employee-engagement-crisis.aspx

The Relationship between Human Capital, Value Creation and Employee Reward
by Peter R. Massingham and Leona Tam of the University of Wollongong

Shawn Achor, *The Happiness Advantage: The Seven Principles of Positive Psychology that Fuel Success and Performance at Work*
http://goodthinkinc.com/resources/books/the-happiness-advantage/

Chapter 8: The Real Cost of Toxic Employees

Michael Housman and Dylan Minor: "Beware those toxic co-workers," *Harvard Gazette*
http://news.harvard.edu/gazette/story/2015/11/those-toxic-co-workers/?utm_source=facebook&utm_medium=social&utm_campaign=hu-facebook-general

"How a Philly firm fired a toxic star performer and sales went up," *Philly.com*
http://www.philly.com/philly/business/20160907_How_a_Philly_firm_fired_a_toxic_star_performer_and_sales_went_up.html

Chapter 9: The Impact of Attitude and Perspective

Nella Bloom: "Monet and Manufacturing – Painting a Picture of Employee Satisfaction"
https://www.linkedin.com/pulse/monet-manufacturing-painting-picture-employee-nella-bloom?trk=prof-post
Institute for Professional Excellence in Coaching (iPEC) – iPEC's Energy Leadership Index (E.L.I.)
http://energyleadership.com/

Chapter 10: The Secret to Innovation: Trust

Brené Brown: *"The Anatomy of Trust"* in her appearance on SuperSoul.TV.
http://www.supersoul.tv/supersoul-sessions/the-anatomy-of-trust

Great Places to Work
https://www.greatplacetowork.com/

https://www.greatplacetowork.com/culture-consulting/financial-performance

https://www.greatplacetowork.com/culture-consulting

Luigi Guiso
http://review.chicagobooth.edu/experts/luigi-guiso

Einaudi Institute for Economics and Finance
http://www.eief.it/

IZA
http://ftp.iza.org/dp8284.pdf

Steven Covey, *The Speed of Trust: The One Thing That Changes Everything*

Monique Caissie: "How Leaders Can Improve Teamwork and Build Trust"
http://www.huffingtonpost.ca/monique-caissie/improve-teamwork_b_8413266.html

Chapter 12: Do You Believe in Miracles? Why Some Teams Succeed While Others Fail

Dr. Janice Presser, TEDx Talk: *"Timing Isn't Everything. Teaming Is."*
https://www.youtube.com/watch?v=aWW36s71Wck

Chapter 13: What Flavor Is Your Kool-Aid
Al Cini: "What's In Your Water Cooler?"
https://www.linkedin.com/pulse/whats-your-water-cooler-al-cini?trk=prof-post

Chapter 14: A Case of Corporate Cultures
Bai's 2017 Super Bowl Commercial
https://youtu.be/HvU2CdzPQf8

Chapter 15: To B, or Not to B

The B Corp Declaration of Interdependence:
https://www.bcorporation.net/what-are-b-corps/the-b-corp-declaration

Good Growth: 26 B Corps on the Inc 5000 List
https://www.bcorporation.net/blog/good-growth-26-b-corps-on-the-inc-5000-list

WorkplaceDynamics' B Corp score card:
https://www.bcorporation.net/community/workplacedynamics

Chapter 17: The New ROI of M&A

Deloitte: *M&A Trends Year-end Report 2016:*
https://www2.deloitte.com/content/dam/Deloitte/us/Documents/mergers-acqisitions/us-ma-mergers-and-acquisitions-trends-2016-year-end-report.pdf

Chapter 18: Build Resilience to Build the Bottom Line
Cheryl Hunter: Media Reel:
https://www.youtube.com/watch?v=mRQ_g0NPSmk&feature=youtu.be

TEDxTalk: Wabi Sabi: The Magnificence of Imperfection:

http://www.cherylhunter.com/tedx/

Chapter 19: The Return on Investment
Frank DiBernardino: *Optimize Human Capital Investments: Make the "Hard" Business Case*
https://www.amazon.com/Optimize-Human-Capital-Investments-Business/dp/1457514664

Jim Collins: *Good to Great*
http://www.jimcollins.com/article_topics/articles/good-to-great.html

Bonus Chapters

I'm including two additional bonus chapters on topics about which I've written. Although these don't tie as directly to the "Return on Individuals" concept as the previous chapters in this book, they do touch on important concepts that support *The NEW ROI: Return on Individuals* and, I believe, offer additional food for thought.

Business Lessons from Beyond the *Shark Tank*

The negotiations end. The deal is struck. Everyone hugs and high-fives. Now what?

In my article, "In the *Shark Tank* It's All about Valuation," I discussed how the Sharks arrive at their valuations. But the show also offers insights into other aspects of business while providing an entertaining glimpse into the world of entrepreneurship and venture capital.

So, what happens to the companies after the deal is struck – or not?

Expanding on the in-show updates, the *Shark Tank* mini-series *Beyond the Tank*, chronicles what happens after the TV appearances, when the entrepreneurs (and Sharks) got down to business. While only a handful of companies are profiled in this mini-series, there are some very practical business lessons to be gleaned from their stories.

1) The Importance of a Consistent Brand

A key element of differentiating from the competition, a powerful brand can illicit loyalty from satisfied customers and potentially allow a company to charge a higher price relative to its competitors.

Brand recognition is built through more than just choosing the right name for a company or designing a memorable logo. A brand symbolizes what the company is known for or wants to be known for and that stems from every product as well as every employee.

Yes, each employee is an embodiment of a company's brand and they deliver the "message" to the customers and suppliers in their words and actions. Think about a time when you called a company's customer service line or walked into a retail location and had to deal with an employee with a poor attitude. How did that make you feel about the company?

The brand is as much a function of corporate culture and a human capital strategy as it is a marketing strategy.

The message of a company's brand must be consistent at every touch-point with the customer.

A brand's message is ultimately associated with the customer experience and if a company is not managing its brand in those terms, consumers will surely let them know about it.

> *"A brand is no longer what we tell the consumer it is – it is what consumers tell each other it is."*
> *~ Scott Cook, co-founder Intuit, Board Member Eby, P&G*

2) "Failure" is a Relative Term

Despite well-scripted and passionate pitches to investors, a company still might not obtain funding. For example, according to *Entrepreneur Media*, only about a half of the pitches on *Shark Tank* resulted in deals, and a large percentage of those deals never actually closed. In the real world, published statistics suggest that far fewer startups actually get funded.

While not getting funded can be a devastating blow, sometimes with the benefit of hindsight, it can become apparent that it wasn't such a bad thing after all. This is because in business, sometimes "No" really means "Not Now" or "You're Not Quite Ready." There are many reasons why investors will pass on a deal and there is an axiom that: "Some of the best deals are the ones that you don't do."

However, this is also true from the company's side of the pitch.

Businesses with great products will fail, but it's how people respond to failure that ultimately determines the final outcome. Resilient determination will often lead people back to the drawing board to get it right (or even better) the next time.

Many great companies and products have gotten it right the second time.

> *"Failures, repeated failures, are finger posts on the road to achievement. One fails forward toward success." ~ C.S. Lewis*

3) Learn to Let Go

An entrepreneur's passion is a critical component to a company's success. That passion produced the vision and the product – as well as providing the determination to persist and overcome adversity. But sometimes that intangible asset, known as passion, can become a liability.

When a company reaches a certain size, it inevitably becomes impossible for the entrepreneur to "wear all of the hats" – or even just their most important hat. When the success of the business prevents the entrepreneur from keeping up with the business, it's time to let go.

Just a little.

Hiring good people to help the entrepreneur is not a bad thing and it doesn't diminish the entrepreneur's contributions. It will actually free them up to do more. They key is to find the right-fit kindred spirits who can bring their creativity and passion to the business. And it's always a good idea to hire someone whose strengths help to mitigate the entrepreneur's weaknesses.

4) $mart Money Can Have a $hort Memory

Friends and family who invest in a business often don't understand what they're buying into and won't likely quibble over valuation. Sometimes the investment is viewed as nothing more than a donation with no expectation of getting their money back. At the other extreme, the investment can be viewed as a lottery ticket with the hope of striking it rich.

In other words, friends and family don't usually have a specific rate of return or timeline in mind when they write the check. However, if the company fails, the founders risk losing their friends and family in addition to their business.

"Smart money" from knowledgeable investors does come with an expectation of a return on the investment – and the timeline for realizing that return can become pretty short, pretty fast, if the business doesn't perform up to expectations. Investors can, and will, cut their losses if it becomes apparent that they will not earn their required rate of return.

With a demonstrated history of execution in its past, however, a company might gain additional credibility and, as a result, a longer runway with investors regarding its ability to perform in the future.

If someone has "done it before," there is often a predisposition to believe that they will do it again. This cuts both ways, however, from the positive as well as the negative perspective, and it will have an impact on the cost of capital.

Final Thoughts

These lessons from "Beyond the *Shark Tank*" are applicable to companies of all sizes and all stages of development – not just startups.

Even the largest publicly traded companies face branding challenges and experience their investors jumping ship if quarterly earnings expectations are missed by the smallest of margins.

Great companies are often founded on great ideas, but great ideas are not a guarantee for raising capital nor is raising capital a guarantee of success.

And yes, in the *Shark Tank* it's still all about valuation.

(https://www.linkedin.com/pulse/shark-tank-its-all-valuation-david-bookbinder-asa)

Five Simple Lessons from 40 Years at the Same Job

Forty years is a long time for anything, let alone holding the same position within the same organization.

Forty years is an especially long time when that organization is a rock band.

What does it take to remain together, be creative, and still like one another after all that time – and what can *you* learn from these guys?

(This article originally appeared at The Huffington Post)

Prelude

When I think about what it takes to remain in a 40-year working relationship, my mind boggles. In a business that is otherwise full of disposables, there aren't many bands that have achieved this type of longevity with this type of success

The band that I refer to is Rush.

Shortly after the release of their self-titled album in 1974, the lineup of Geddy Lee, Alex Lifeson, and Neil Peart have recorded and toured as the triumvirate known as Rush.

Rush is known for their extended-length songs, complex time signatures, and concept albums. As a result, they weren't considered radio-friendly, and it's been said that no one has ever been overheard whistling a Rush tune.

The band, often referred to as a Canadian "power trio," has been characterized in the genres of hard rock and progressive rock, although their sound evolved to include a variety of additional elements including new wave and even reggae.

Their 40-year career has included record sales in excess of 40 million units, sold-out world-wide concert tours, a star on the Hollywood Walk of Fame, and their induction into the Rock and Roll Hall of Fame in 2013. (Finally!)

Rush has also gotten visibility from their appearance in the movie *I Love You Man* as well as on the *Colbert Report*.

Lessons Learned

I've seen Rush perform live countless times since the Hemispheres tour in 1978, and I've had the pleasure of meeting Alex and Geddy all-too-briefly before their 30th Anniversary tour. I can tell you that these are a couple of the most humble, unassuming, down-to-earth guys that you'd ever meet.

In the sections that follow, I use the word "you" to represent either you-the-individual or you-the-company, depending on your particular perspective, in sharing some of the lessons that can we learn from the band called Rush.

"All the world's indeed a stage and we are merely players" – Limelight

1. It Takes a Great Team

Think about your two favorite people. Now imagine working with them, living with them, doing almost everything with them for say... 40 years.

I know, right?

The respect, chemistry, and bond that has to exist for Alex, Geddy, and Neil to accomplish what they have – and still like each other – over the period of time that they have been together is nothing short of remarkable.

From an interview at *Grammy.com*, according to Geddy Lee: "Most of the time the biggest concern we have is, who is going to say something funnier? Where we get into one-upmanship is in the comedy department, not the music department. I think those things combined have really helped keep this band going."

What usually destroys a band are creative differences and personality clashes. Rush was able to avoid both.

Neil Peart, in an interview with *Power Windows*, said: "It was most important for each of us to be equal in input and output – each of us has to pull the same amount, musically, in composition and in every sense of being in the band. All of us have to pull together. It seems to me that's the only way you can have a truly creative aggregate of people is if they're all contributing in different ways."

To build an organization that can withstand the test of time requires teamwork. And within that team, it is not only imperative to have the right people on the team, it is imperative that each team member has a clearly defined role and that there is trust within the team to inspire innovation. It is this type of culture that fosters collaboration and communication.

It is this type of culture that fosters success.

"Glittering prizes and endless compromises, shatter the illusion of integrity" – The Spirit of Radio

2. Don't Give Up!

When your lead singer's vocals are described in an album review as "snip-and-clip day at the kennel," you need to develop thick skin and ignore the critics that are trying to bring you down.

But sometimes life requires that you overcome hardships that go far beyond that of just a bad review.

Rush "disappeared" for a five-year period in the late-90s due to Neil Peart suffering the tragic loss of his daughter in a car accident, followed by losing his wife to cancer in a little less than a year after that. Rather than get another drummer to perform in Neil's absence, Alex and Geddy remained steadfast that there was no Rush without Neil.

Overcoming this type of adversity is incomprehensible, and no one would have second-guessed the band if they never returned. But they did return. (More on this below.)

Dealing with the critics is easy by comparison. And there will always be critics. These "critics" can be external forces, but sometimes your worst critic of all is you. You must ignore the doubtful self-talk that comes from the fear of failure, or the uncertainty of starting over, and keep pushing on.

Earlier in the book, we discussed the importance of Grit in determining one's success; these guys personify Grit.

"I can't stop thinking big, I can't stop thinking big." – Caravan

3. Be Humble

When you achieve a certain level of success, however you define success, it is important that you not let it go to your head.

You see it all the time in sports, music, business – everywhere. Sometimes it's the guy "who was born on third base but thought he hit a triple." Sometimes it's the gal who you "knew when..." who now has no time for you... or starts acting "differently."

By any standard, Rush has achieved success. Record sales, concert tours, longevity, recognition by their peers. It all adds up to a successful career.

But through it all, they have remained humble. And while they have always taken their craft very seriously, they've never taken themselves too seriously.

According to guitarist, Alex Lifeson in a *Rolling Stone* interview: "I guess we've been around for so long, we have fans all over the place, and they're getting older and more influential. I guess you get movie directors and doctors and writers, and suddenly your name comes up in a film or documentary."

Being humble about their achievements, or even making fun of themselves, Rush has always been authentic and grateful.

It is these qualities that have helped them to build and grow what has been described as a cult-like fan base that has supported them over the years.

It's no different with people in any business or any aspect of life for that matter. It's really a pretty simple concept: nobody likes an a** hole. Don't be an a** hole.

"If you choose not to decide, you still have made a choice." - Freewill

4. Connect with the Customer
What drew me to Rush initially were the lyrics of the songs. They were not like the other bands – their lyrics were more... cerebral.

And the sound... how did three guys do all of that?

Early in the history of Rush, it was a rarity to see women at Rush concerts. But over the years, the Rush fan-base has grown to be a diverse mix of men, women, and even kids, as parents introduced their children to their band.

To not only maintain but grow a customer base over the years requires several things:

The product is of a consistently high-quality. The musicianship of Rush is that of virtuosity, with each band member largely considered to be one of the best to ever play their respective instruments. Neil Peart is, in fact, considered by many to be the best drummer of all time.

The customer experience is great. Rush has never skimped on a live performance. According to Peart: "Live shows were always religion for us. We never played a show – whether it was in front of 15 people or 15,000 – where it wasn't everything we had that night." Given the level of technical difficulty required to perform many of their songs, the bar has always been set at a high level for them to execute. The stage shows and background videos always enhanced the experience. Give the people what they want.

The brand inspires loyalty. Always innovative and authentic, Rush has connected with its "customers" like no other band. Previously I alluded to the band's "comeback" after their hiatus. The band had built so much goodwill and loyalty over the preceding years that upon returning to the stage after a long absence, Rush was overwhelmingly welcomed back by their fans.

Brand loyalty inspires brand passion. If you've ever met someone who claims to be a Rush fan, you know exactly what I'm talking about. There is a passionate loyalty and enthusiasm in this customer base that might only be rivaled by the folks who sleep outside awaiting the release of a new gizmo. These are your brand ambassadors.

"The more that things change, the more they stay the same." – *Circumstances*

5. Learn To Adapt

Fashion styles will change. Hair styles will change. Musical tastes will change.

So will technology, the economy, and customer preferences.

One of the great keys to success is being able to adapt yourself, your company, or your product to the changing times.

Reinvention for the sake of keeping up is only a part of the story though. You also need to have the ability to see ahead of the curve to maintain or acquire a leadership position. Anticipating those trends requires a strategic vision.

Rush changed with the times while always remaining true to their core principles. From wearing kimonos to wearing skinny neck ties, the band always had its place on the musical hierarchy. While other bands disappeared from the scene with the changing times, Rush endured.

As Geddy puts it: "I guess, we were people who just dedicated to trying to get better."

If you aren't able to anticipate and adapt with changing times, changing environments, or changing preferences, you will be left behind.

Exit Stage Left

Whether you are a fan of Rush or not, there are many lessons that can be gleaned from their career. Even if you're not a fan, you probably know at least one of their songs, the iconic Tom Sawyer.

I've shared this song on my blog on this topic. So shut your door, turn up the speakers, and air-drum your way down memory lane.
(https://www.linkedin.com/pulse/5-simple-lessons-from-40-years-same-job-dave-bookbinder)

Bonus Chapters

About the Author

Dave Bookbinder is a corporate finance executive with a focus on valuation. Known as a collaborative consultant, Dave has served thousands of client companies of all sizes and industries.

Working closely with business owners, CFOs, Controllers, and CEOs, Dave strives to build relationships that add value for the long term.

Dave has conducted valuations of the securities and intangible assets of public and private companies for various purposes including acquisition, divestiture, financial reporting, stock-based compensation, fairness and solvency opinions, reorganizations, recapitalizations, estate planning, S-Corp. conversion, exit strategy, succession planning, and regulatory compliance.

Among the many types of intellectual property and intangible assets that Dave has valued are human capital assets.

During his career, Dave has also provided financial advisory services to client companies for strategic planning purposes including buy-side and sell-side M&A, private placements of senior debt, securitization of lease and loan receivables, and pre-acquisition purchase price allocation analysis.

Dave holds a bachelor's degree in Economics from Temple University and a master's degree in Finance from Drexel University.

Dave is an Accredited Senior Appraiser (ASA) in Business Valuation with the American Society of Appraisers and also holds the designation of CEIV, Certified in Entity and Intangible Valuations. He is also a business section contributor for *The HuffPost*.

Dave's teams have been recognized by a variety of independent organizations for excellence in Valuation Consulting. Dave was also personally recognized by *SmartCEO* Magazine with an award for Executive Management, and he is also a two-time recipient of the Morris Groner Award for Entrepreneurship. Dave is most proud of the multiple awards he's received for fostering the Best Corporate Culture.

"As someone who's regularly involved in the valuation of intangible assets, I'm often asked which intangible asset is the most valuable to a company. I've always believed that it's the people."

For future insights and articles, connect with Dave on LinkedIn, like him on Facebook, follow him on Twitter, #NEWROI and subscribe to his blog at HuffPost.